TABLE OF CONTENTS

Introduction   ix

About the Author   xv

My To-Do Checklists   xvii

My Action Checklists   xxiii

Chapter 1: Do First Things First   1

  First Things Action Checklists   9

    Burial   9

    Celebration of Life   11

    Charities   13

    Cremation   14

    Donation of Organs and Tissues   15

    Entombment   16

    Ethical Will/Legacy Documents   17

    Funeral or Memorial Service Arrangements   18

    Funeral Expenses   21

    Obituary   23

    Persons to Contact   24

    Pet Care   27

    Whole Body Donation   28

    First Things: Other   29

Chapter 2: Get Organized for What Comes Next   31

Get Organized Action Checklists   *35*

Personal History of the Deceased   35

Children and Grandchildren   39

Parents   44

Brothers and Sisters   45

Grandparents   52

Stepgrandparents   54

Aunts, Uncles, and Cousins   55

Stepparents   58

Stepbrothers and Stepsisters   59

Records to Locate   61

Get Organized: Other   67

Chapter 3: Build a Team You Can Rely On   69

Build a Team Action Checklists   *75*

Assigned Tasks   75

Financial Professionals   78

Lawyers   80

Build a Team: Other   82

Chapter 4: Apply for Survivors' Benefits   83

Survivors' Benefits Action Checklists   *97*

Pensions   97

Social Security Benefits   99

Veterans' Benefits   100

Workers' Compensation   101

Survivors' Benefits: Other   102

Chapter 5: Find Out What's at the Bank — 103

Banking Action Checklists — *109*

Certificates of Deposit — 109

Checking Accounts — 111

Credit Union Accounts — 113

Safe-Deposit Boxes — 114

Savings Accounts — 116

Savings Bonds — 117

Banking: Other — 118

Chapter 6: Learn What's Available in Investments — 119

Investments Checklists — *127*

Bonds — 127

Money Market Funds and Accounts — 129

Mutual Funds — 130

Stocks — 131

Individual Retirement Accounts (IRAs) — 132

Roth IRA — 133

401(k), 457(b), 403(b), and TSP Plans — 134

SIMPLE IRA — 135

SEP IRA — 136

Investments: Other — 137

Chapter 7: Check on Insurance Benefits — 139

Insurance Action Checklists — *151*

Annuities — 151

Automobile Insurance — 153

Health, Disability, and Medicare Health Insurance — 155

Homeowners' Insurance 158

Life Insurance 159

Other Residence Insurance 160

Other Vehicle Insurance 161

Insurance: Other 163

Chapter 8: Stay Put in Your Home for Now **165**

Real Estate Action Checklists *173*

Commercial or Rental Property 173

Condominium 174

Farmland 175

Rental Agreements 176

Residence 177

Time-share 178

Real Estate: Other 179

Chapter 9: Pay Debts **181**

Pay Debts Action Checklists *189*

Commercial Property Debts 189

Condominium 191

Credit Cards 192

Credit Reporting Companies 195

Farmland 196

Personal Debts 198

Residence 199

Time-share 201

Pay Debts: Other 202

Chapter 10: Sort through the Stuff and Papers   **203**

   Sort Stuff Action Checklists   *213*

       Passwords   213

       Rewards Accounts   216

       Sort Stuff: Other   219

Chapter 11: Get Ready for Probate   **221**

   Get Ready for Probate Action Checklists   *231*

       Codicils   231

       Gifts   232

       Letter of Instruction   233

       Living Trust   234

       Will   235

       Get Ready for Probate: Other   236

Chapter 12: Take Care of Yourself   **237**

INTRODUCTION

Someone in the family just died. On top of the emotional crisis of losing a loved one, multiple decisions have to be made. What about the funeral? Where and when will the memorial service be held? What goes in the obituary, and who's going to write it? Who needs to be notified, and who has the phone numbers? These questions are just a few of those to be answered in the first day.

In the days following the death, yet more questions have to be answered. Who is going to take care of the dog? Where are the keys? What's in the safe-deposit box? When do we have to clean out the home? Have the utilities been paid for the month? Who has the ATM card? Has anyone notified the bank? Where is the Social Security check deposited?

I have assembled this book, *ABA/AARP Checklist for Family Survivors: A Guide to Practical and Legal Matters When Someone You Love Dies*, for family members who may be struggling to answer these and many more questions. You may be a spouse, a son, a sister, or a grandchild. In the days and weeks after a death, one or all of you need to take steps to wrap up the personal and financial affairs of the loved one who died.

This book is not about probate. In fact, that topic is not covered until Chapter 11 and then only in a general way so that you know what to anticipate. It is about settling an estate in the broadest terms. You'll find no legal advice, but you'll learn legal reasons, implications, and complications.

The checklists in Chapter 1 walk you through the process of arranging for a funeral and burial. Understand why it is important to follow the wishes of your loved one. Track down any preneed contract in which some of the costs have already been paid. You'll find tips on writing an obituary and developing a visual tribute.

Chapters 2 and 3 help you start to get organized for the detective work that lies ahead. You'll find suggestions for setting up filing systems to organize what could be an avalanche of names, phones numbers, web addresses, messages, instructions, letters, and e-mails for all the people and entities you need to contact. Use the checklists in Chapter 2 to organize all the family relationships. Assembling this information has two purposes. You'll use it to know what family members need to be notified of the death and whom to mention in the obituary. Later on, when it comes time to settle the estate, the executor needs to know who needs to be notified of the probate of the estate. If there's no will, the executor will also use this family tree to identify all the possible heirs.

The Records to Locate checklist in Chapter 2 puts in one place all the documents and other important information you may need to find. Once you've found each item, record on the checklist where it's located. Don't be put off by the length of this list. If the item doesn't apply to your loved one, just check it off. It's comprehensive so that you can make sure you don't overlook something.

It's more than a one-person show to settle an estate. It takes a team and teamwork. Use the Assigned Tasks checklist in Chapter 3 to keep track of who in the family is going to do what. When someone offers to help, you'll have a ready list of what needs to be done, who's doing it, and when he or she needs to finish the task. Relying on family can be either a blessing or trouble, depending on your family. When working with some family members, you may need to dig deep for your best negotiating skills. Learn tips on setting boundaries for family discussions. You most likely will need to call upon lawyers, financial advisors, or tax preparers. You'll find guidance on what you need to look for when selecting this advice or assistance.

The death of a loved one can have significant financial consequences to the surviving family members. When the paychecks stop coming in, the family quickly needs to find out what survivors' benefits are available to supplement the family's income. Chapter 4 walks you through all the various benefits that may be available. If the loved one was a veteran, there are a number of possible benefits to apply for. The Veterans Administration has benefits related to the funeral and burial of the veteran. The surviving family members may also be eligible for financial assistance.

Social Security also can provide financial help to eligible family members. In addition to the government programs, financial support for the family can come from pension plans or retirement savings accounts that the loved one set aside during working years. Use the Action Checklists in Chapter 4 to identify government, pension, and retirement benefits to stabilize family resources. Start with the Survivors' Benefits Quick Tips for a handy list of what you need to do to apply for each of these benefits.

Chapter 5 tells you what you need to do about any bank accounts. First, you need to locate all the various accounts; then, you should notify each bank of the death. The type of account and whose name is on it can make a big difference in what happens to the money. You'll find explanations of account types and what you need to take with you when you go to the bank. While at the bank, you will also want to learn how to access the safe-deposit box. The box may contain important documents or valuables that need to be inventoried.

Your loved one may also have left an investment portfolio, such as mutual funds, stocks, bonds, or other types of investment or retirement accounts. These assets need to be identified, valued, inventoried, and distributed. In Chapter 6, you will find out about all the different types of investments and what needs to be done to properly distribute or reinvest the money in the account. Depending on type of investment, the rules can differ. Who inherits the particular investment depends on how the asset was held. It is critical to know whether an investment is held jointly with another person or whether beneficiaries are named.

All the many kinds of insurance are discussed in Chapter 7. You may need to deal with life insurance, health insurance, homeowners' insurance, and vehicle insurance. You'll need to find all the various policies, notify the companies, and then take the various steps required to receive the proceeds, cancel the policy, or reestablish the policy in a different name. Life insurance proceeds need to be distributed to the named beneficiaries. You'll work with the health insurance company to pay any medical claims related to the last illness or injury. If you were on your loved one's group insurance plan, you may need to explore options to get health insurance for yourself and your family. Home and cars should continue to be insured, so it's important to notify the insurance company of any change in ownership or use. Use the sample letter in this chapter to notify insurance companies of the death.

Where your loved one was living at the time of death dictates what steps need to be taken about possession or ownership of the property. Chapter 8 explores what happens to real property, be it an apartment, house, condominium, or time-share. What you'll need to do depends on the type of living arrangement. If your loved one had been living in a nursing home or assisted living facility, it may be relatively easy to give notice and remove all the personal items. If he or she had been living alone in a rental, check the lease for how much time the family has to give notice to vacate, clean up the apartment, and get the security deposit returned. If the loved one had been living at home, what happens to ownership of the home depends on how the property was titled. When a spouse dies, the home may no longer feel right. Nevertheless, staying put may be the best choice for now.

Debts and what to do about them are covered in Chapter 9. You'll find out how to know what debts need to be paid and don't need to be paid as well as a caution on dealing with aggressive debt collectors. To prevent identity thieves from using your loved one's personal information to open fraudulent accounts and rack up bills, be sure to notify the credit reporting bureaus of the death.

Just about everyone has stuff. When a person dies, someone has to make decisions about what to do with personal items. It could be a couple of suitcases or a whole house full of stuff. Knowing how best to deal with the personal things can be one of the most difficult tasks for survivors. It can be emotionally devastating to part with items that bring back wonderful memories of times together. On the other hand, family members are known to get into critical disagreements over knick-knacks. At all times, the wishes of the loved one need to be followed, but sometimes those wishes are not very clear. Use the What to Keep and When to Shred checklist in Chapter 10 for what you can get rid of and how long you need to keep important papers.

Not only do people have tangible stuff, they also have virtual possession. The online world includes social media accounts, electronic books, stored music, bank accounts, and travel rewards. Getting access to all these online accounts and assets requires usernames and passwords. If your loved one didn't leave a list of accounts and passwords, you could be facing a big cleanup job. Chapter 10 also helps you through this maze on the ground and in the cloud.

Chapters 1 through 10 are about gathering information and taking the preliminary steps to settle an estate, including small details that need attention and big decisions that have to be made, no matter the size of the estate. Chapter 11 looks at the formalities of the probate process to officially close an estate. Large or small estate, will or no will, trust or no trust, there are legal requirements that must be followed when dealing with the assets that belong to someone else. Laws about titling assets, distributing retirement accounts, paying out insurance proceeds, managing assets in trust, receiving benefits, and opening safe-deposit boxes are in place to protect the interests of the decedent. It might seem that dealing with government representatives, bank officials, courts, insurance companies, and creditors is a never-ending hassle. The need for death certificates, documents, letters, notices, telephone calls, and e-mails can seem like barriers set up to complicate your life. The key to over-coming these frustrations is to focus on making sure you are honoring the memory and the wishes of your loved one with every step you take or decision you make.

The final chapter focuses on you. Stress is a natural reaction to the death of a loved one, but it can be harmful to your own health and well-being. Take care of yourself, even set aside some time to pamper yourself. Chapter 12 provides stress-relieving tips and suggestions for support.

My first book, *ABA Checklist for Family Heirs*, helps people get their own affairs in order before they die. By using checklists similar to those in this book, anyone can organize information about their family history, financial affairs, and wishes for the end of life. Doing so is a gift to other family members so that they will more easily know what the person had, be able to locate the important documentation they need, and feel confident that they are carrying out the loved ones' wishes. This book is for those who have not had the benefit of that gift. Once you have worked through these checklists and know what it's like to settle another's estate, get a copy of *ABA Checklist for Family Heirs* for yourself so that you can give that gift to your family.

How to Use This Book

ABA/AARP Checklist for Family Survivors is not a book that you just sit down and read. Use it as a guide or workbook to help you understand what you need to know and what you need to do following a loved one's death.

Each chapter starts with a personal **To-Do Checklist** that you use to identify the steps you need to take and the information you need to gather. For each item on the checklist, you will find an explanation of the steps, why you need to gather the information, and tips on where to look for it. At the end of each chapter are **Action Checklists** where you record and organize all the details.

To give you an overview of the many topics covered, you will probably want to start by looking through the To-Do Checklist and Action Checklist summaries starting at pages xvii and xxiii, respectively. In your first run through the checklists, check off the items that don't apply to your loved one's circumstances. Your loved one may not own many of the assets listed on the checklists. If so, indicate that they do not apply and move on. By going through each checklist, you may quickly learn that there are lots of details you don't have to worry about and can be assured that you aren't overlooking something. You may find that you'll want to start with a single section or checklist that is easy for you to accomplish.

Check off each item on the To-Do Checklist as you complete that step. Even though you might not have all the answers at first, take the time to find them. Some information will take extra thought or research. Once you've gathered the information, you need a place to keep it organized. Record what you've learned in that Action Checklist. Feel free to modify the checklists according to your family's circumstances.

Paper or Plastic

You have the choice to write in the book or use your computer. This book is designed for you to write in, but you can also fill in the forms by using the CD-ROM included in the back cover. With the CD-ROM, it is very easy to fill out the checklists and make changes so that they are up-to-date. Using the CD also makes it easy for you to share collected information with others in your family as you work together to get everything done. Note in this book the file or folder name where you have downloaded the forms so that others can access them. As you complete a chapter online, you may want to print a copy and place the pages in a three-ring binder.

A Word of Caution

You are assembling a great deal of very personal information that, in the wrong hands, could be used to your loved one's disadvantage. Unfortunately, there are unscrupulous people who do not have your family's best interests in mind. They may even be people that you believe you should be able to trust. Although they may not admit it, some relatives may be more concerned about their own interests than in your loved one's wants. Be cautious with the information you're collecting and who you are sharing it with. The nosy neighbor, the distant relative, or the casual friend may not be able to keep such very private information confidential.

ABOUT THE AUTHOR

Sally Balch Hurme, J.D., is currently a project advisor with the AARP Health Law Education team. In her more than 20 years at AARP, she has advocated on a wide range of issues, including consumer fraud, financial exploitation, elder abuse, surrogate decision making, advance care planning, predatory mortgage lending, health care fraud, and financial security. She is well recognized as an elder law advocate who is quoted frequently in national media, including the *Wall Street Journal*, *USA Today*, CNN.com, *Money*, *Kiplinger's Retirement Report*, NPR, and *AARP The Magazine*.

Although she has written more than 20 law review articles on elder law topics, Hurme has focused her professional career on explaining the law so that everyone can understand it. She has lectured in Australia, Japan, the Netherlands, Germany, Spain, Italy, Czech Republic, Great Britain, and Moldova on elder abuse and surrogate decision making. She is also in demand as a speaker, having given more than 100 presentations on elder law topics in at least 40 states.

For the past two decades, Hurme's volunteer commitment has focused on the rights of adults with diminished capacity and the reform of guardianship policy and procedures. She has served multiple terms on the boards of the National Guardianship Association and the Center for Guardianship Certification, where she has been instrumental in developing standards for guardians and criteria to improve professional competency. She is the past chair of the National Guardianship Network, a collaboration of ten national organizations working to improve guardianship. In addition, Hurme was a key planner of both the 2011 Third National Guardianship Summit and the 2014 Third World Congress on Adult Guardianship. She was an advisor to the Uniform Law Commission in the drafting of the uniform guardianship jurisdiction act, which has been adopted in 39 states. She was a member of U.S. State Department delegation to the Hague Conference on Private International Law that drafted the International Convention on the Protection of Incapacitated Adults. In 2008, Hurme was honored by the National College of Probate Judges with the William Treat Award for excellence in probate law.

Hurme started her legal career as a partner in a private law firm, gained valuable experience serving older clients as a legal services attorney, and served as a magistrate in Alexandria, Virginia. She spent three years as an attorney advisor with the U.S. Department of Justice Office of Intelligence Policy and Review. She then returned to elder law advocacy as an assistant staff attorney with the American Bar Association Commission on Law and Aging before moving to AARP.

Hurme taught elder law as an adjunct professor at the George Washington University Law School for eight years and taught legal research and writing at the Washington College of Law for ten years. She is a long-term member of the National Academy of Elder Law Attorneys and the Virginia and District of Columbia bars. Hurme was a member of the Discipline and Ethics Commission of the Certified Financial Planners Board of Standards. She serves a member of the Board of Governors for the Stuart Hall School in Staunton, Virginia.

She received her B.A. from Newcomb College of Tulane University, New Orleans, Louisiana, and received her J.D. cum laude from the Washington College of Law, American University, Washington, D.C. She lives in Alexandria, Virginia, but enjoys getaway time at her farm near Shepherdstown, West Virginia.

MY TO-DO CHECKLISTS

Here's an overview of what this book helps you do.

Chapter 1: Do First Things First

- ❏ Authorize donation of organs or tissue
- ❏ Contact the medical school for body bequeathal
- ❏ Contact the funeral home for removal of the body
- ❏ Make the funeral arrangements
- ❏ Research the costs of funerals
- ❏ Arrange for the burial
- ❏ Notify friends and family of the death and funeral arrangements
- ❏ Ensure the safety of the home and pets
- ❏ Maintain lists of helpers and help needed
- ❏ Arrange for a visual tribute
- ❏ Write and submit the obituary
- ❏ Locate and share legacy information such as an ethical will

Chapter 2: Get Organized for What Comes Next

- ❏ Set up a filing system
- ❏ Make copies of all documents
- ❏ Keep notes of conversations
- ❏ Track down family history

Chapter 3: Build a Team You Can Rely On

- ❑ Know your family
- ❑ Understand the stages of grief
- ❑ Head off family discord
- ❑ Draw on special talents
- ❑ Identify the need for a lawyer
- ❑ Find a financial advisor
- ❑ Check on the background of any financial professional

Chapter 4: Apply for Survivors' Benefits

- ❑ Notify Social Security of the death
- ❑ Apply for Social Security survivors' benefits
- ❑ Get copies of birth certificate
- ❑ Get copies of marriage license
- ❑ Get copies of divorce decree
- ❑ Apply for the veteran's burial benefits
- ❑ Get a copy of military service record (DD 214)
- ❑ Request a burial flag
- ❑ Request a veteran's burial
- ❑ Request a veteran's headstone
- ❑ Request military honors
- ❑ Get reimbursement for funeral or burial expenses
- ❑ Apply for veterans' benefits as a survivor
- ❑ Apply for education benefits
- ❑ Apply for workers' compensation survivor benefits
- ❑ Identify all available pension benefits
- ❑ Take disbursements from 401(k) retirement plans
- ❑ Take disbursements from individual retirement accounts

Chapter 5: Find Out What's at the Bank

- ❑ Notify all banks or credit unions of the death and provide a copy of the death certificate
- ❑ Assemble account numbers and determine PINs, ATM passwords, and online banking usernames and passwords
- ❑ Review how bank accounts are titled
- ❑ Document your authority
- ❑ Determine what to do about direct deposits and payments
- ❑ Redeem all savings bonds
- ❑ Access and inventory any safe-deposit boxes

Chapter 6: Learn What's Available in Investments

- ❑ Understand the different types of investments
- ❑ Get tax advice on how to take distribution of and manage any sums you inherit from a 401(k) or IRA
- ❑ Identify all investment accounts
- ❑ Promptly contact any investment professionals so that accounts can be valued as of the date of death for tax purposes
- ❑ Identify all retirement plans
- ❑ Contact all employers and former employers for information on any retirement savings accounts
- ❑ Search for any unclaimed money

Chapter 7: Check on Insurance Benefits

- ❑ Review terms of all insurance policies
- ❑ Locate all insurance policies (life, care, homeowners, etc.)
- ❑ Contact the insurance company for instructions on how to file a claim for annuity or life insurance benefits
- ❑ Determine your health insurance options
- ❑ Get help paying Medicare costs
- ❑ Notify any health insurance plans

❑ Notify the vehicle insurance company so that there is coverage until the vehicle is sold or transferred

❑ Contact the insurance company to ensure that the home and its contents are properly insured

❑ Make sure that a homeowners' or renters' policy remains in effect if no one is going to be living in the home

Chapter 8: Stay Put in Your Home for Now

❑ Secure all property for safety

❑ Assemble copies of the deeds or other documentation of ownership to all real estate

❑ Obtain a copy of the condominium's master deed and association documents

❑ Review how the property is titled

❑ Obtain a copy of any trust documents

❑ Obtain a copy of any time-share contracts

❑ Consult with an attorney about the need to change the title to any property if you are a surviving joint owner

❑ Check out the rental agreement

❑ Stay put for now

Chapter 9: Pay Debts

❑ Assemble documentation of all bills and credit card accounts

❑ Determine if there are any other types of debts

❑ Notify all credit card companies

❑ Send a copy of the death certificate to each credit reporting company

❑ Determine how much debt is due

❑ Get credit in your own name if you held joint accounts

❑ Take care of the home mortgage or rent

❑ Make arrangements to pay off the reverse mortgage

❑ Pay attention to any vehicle liens

Chapter 10: Sort through the Stuff and Papers

❑ Take photographs of rooms, cabinets, and closets

❑ Identify the valuables and their value

❑ Respect the wishes of your loved one

❑ Set up a system to distribute personal items

❑ Shred the paper

❑ Consider estate sales, garage sales, and donations to charities

❑ Recycle with care

❑ Manage digital assets

Chapter 11: Get Ready for Probate

❑ Inventory all the assets

❑ Determine how assets are owned

❑ Know what to do if there's a living trust

❑ Follow any letter of instruction

❑ Get acquainted with the probate process

❑ Locate the will

❑ Document any major financial gifts

❑ Engage the services of an attorney

Chapter 12: Take Care of Yourself

❑ Manage your stress

❑ Get support

❑ Plan a break

❑ Take care of your health

❑ Organize your own life

MY ACTION CHECKLISTS

Check off the boxes when you've completed each checklist.

Chapter 1: Do First Things First

- ❑ Burial
- ❑ Celebration of Life
- ❑ Charities
- ❑ Cremation
- ❑ Donation of Organs and Tissues
- ❑ Entombment
- ❑ Ethical Will/Legacy Documents
- ❑ Funeral or Memorial Service Arrangements
- ❑ Funeral Expenses
- ❑ Obituary
- ❑ Persons to Contact
- ❑ Pet Care
- ❑ Whole Body Donation
- ❑ First Things: Other

Chapter 2: Get Organized for What Comes Next

- ❑ Personal History of the Deceased
- ❑ Children and Grandchildren
- ❑ Parents

❑ Brothers and Sisters

❑ Grandparents

❑ Stepgrandparents

❑ Aunts, Uncles, and Cousins

❑ Steppparents

❑ Stepbrothers and Stepsisters

❑ Records to Locate

❑ Get Organized: Other

Chapter 3: Build a Team You Can Rely On

❑ Assigned Tasks

❑ Financial Professionals

❑ Lawyers

❑ Build a Team: Other

Chapter 4: Apply for Survivors' Benefits

❑ Pensions

❑ Social Security Benefits

❑ Veterans' Benefits

❑ Workers' Compensation

❑ Survivors' Benefits: Other

Chapter 5: Find Out What's at the Bank

❑ Certificates of Deposit

❑ Checking Accounts

❑ Credit Union Accounts

❑ Safe-Deposit Boxes

❑ Savings Accounts

❑ Savings Bonds

❑ Banking: Other

Chapter 6: Learn What's Available in Investments

- ❑ Bonds
- ❑ Money Market Funds and Accounts
- ❑ Mutual Funds
- ❑ Stocks
- ❑ Individual Retirement Accounts (IRAs)
- ❑ Roth IRA
- ❑ 401(k), 457(b), 403(b), and TSP Plans
- ❑ SIMPLE IRA
- ❑ SEP IRA
- ❑ Investments: Other

Chapter 7: Check on Insurance Benefits

- ❑ Annuities
- ❑ Automobile Insurance
- ❑ Health, Disability, and Medicare Health Insurance
- ❑ Homeowners' Insurance
- ❑ Life Insurance
- ❑ Other Residence Insurance
- ❑ Other Vehicle Insurance
- ❑ Insurance: Other

Chapter 8: Stay Put in Your Home for Now

- ❑ Commercial or Rental Property
- ❑ Condominium
- ❑ Farmland
- ❑ Residence
- ❑ Time-share
- ❑ Real Estate: Other

Chapter 9: Pay the Debts

- ❏ Commercial Property Debts
- ❏ Condominium
- ❏ Credit Cards
- ❏ Credit Reporting Companies
- ❏ Farm Land
- ❏ Personal Debts
- ❏ Residence
- ❏ Time-share
- ❏ Pay Debts: Other

Chapter 10: Sort through the Stuff and Paper

- ❏ Passwords
- ❏ Rewards Accounts
- ❏ Sort Stuff: Other

Chapter 11: Get Ready for Probate

- ❏ Codicils
- ❏ Gifts
- ❏ Letter of Instruction
- ❏ Living Trust
- ❏ Will
- ❏ Get Ready for Probate: Other

CHAPTER 1
DO FIRST THINGS FIRST

Whether the death of your loved one comes suddenly or whether it is anticipated after a long illness, the realization that death has come brings a tidal wave of emotions. Some people may feel suspended in space or don't know how they will manage the next few hours, let alone the months and years to come. The numbness you may feel is a protective response to the shock of the loss. In this stage of grief, you may feel overwhelmed by the number of decisions you must now make. On the other hand, taking care of the final details that family members must attend to may be a way to distract yourself from the pain and start working through the grieving process.

You'll be called on to make a great number of decisions in the first few days after someone dies. Ideally, you had the opportunity to talk with your loved one about his or her wishes for funeral or burial. Even if you did not have that chance, you'll want to reflect on what you know about your loved one's preferences. You may recall comments that he or she made when dealing with the death of another about how the funeral details should have been handled. Look for a letter of instruction with details about plans your loved one made for care after death. You'll want to make decisions as closely as possible to what your loved one would want.

Use these checklists to get an overview of the decisions you'll need to make. You might be able to delegate some tasks to others, so review Chapter 3 about assembling a support team you can count on. You should rely on family and friends to give you guidance and assistance. Be sure to take people up on their offers to help.

My to-do checklist

Done	Need to Do	
❏	❏	Authorize donation of organs or tissue
❏	❏	Contact the medical school for body bequeathal
❏	❏	Contact the funeral home for removal of the body
❏	❏	Make the funeral arrangements

❏	❏	Research the costs of funerals
❏	❏	Arrange for the burial
❏	❏	Notify friends and family of the death and funeral arrangements
❏	❏	Ensure the safety of the home and pets
❏	❏	Maintain lists of helpers and help needed
❏	❏	Arrange for a visual tribute
❏	❏	Write and submit the obituary
❏	❏	Locate and share legacy information such as an ethical will
❏	❏	Complete the checklists for Chapter 1

First things action checklists

The Action Checklists in this chapter are set out in the following order:

- *Burial*
- *Celebration of Life*
- *Charities*
- *Cremation*
- *Donation of Organs and Tissues*
- *Entombment*
- *Ethical Will/Legacy Documents*
- *Funeral or Memorial Service Arrangements*
- *Funeral Expenses*
- *Obituary*
- *Persons to Contact*
- *Pet Care*
- *Whole Body Donation*
- *First Things: Other*

✓ Authorize donation of organs or tissue

Organ and tissue donations have saved or improved thousands of lives, yet there is always a very long list of patients waiting for organ transplants. According to the U.S. Department of Health and Human Services, 18 patients die each day because of the shortage of available donated organs.

You need to check to see if your loved one gave consent to be a donor by signing an organ or tissue donation card. In some states, this consent can be as simple as a statement on a driver's license. All states have an organ donation registry. You can find your state's registry as well as other information about the donor process at www.organdonor.gov/. On my Virginia driver's license, a small heart under my picture indicates that I'm on the Virginia registry as someone who has consented to be a donor. If your loved one had not indicated his or her consent to be a donor ahead of time, the local organ procurement organization will contact the next of kin for consent to make the donation.

Most organ donations are made immediately after a person has been declared brain dead following severe head trauma, heart attack, or stroke. Donated organs must be removed and transplanted within hours of the death, whereas tissue donations of corneas, heart valves, skin, and bones can be preserved and stored in tissue banks. The organs or tissues are removed through a surgical procedure. After the removal procedures, the body will be prepared as normal for the funeral and can be buried or cremated as though it were intact. The family will not have any expenses related to the donation.

✓ Contact the medical school for body bequeathal

If your loved one made arrangements in advance for a whole body donation to a medical school or research facility, you need to contact the school or research entity as soon as you know of the death. The facility will have specific instructions for how to transfer the body. Typically, the facility will cremate the body at no expense and deliver the ashes as instructed.

✓ Contact the funeral home for removal of the body

You will need to decide what will be done with the body after death. Choices include being embalmed to delay decomposition of the body, a natural burial without embalming, burial in a coffin in a cemetery or in a crypt in a mausoleum, or cremation. If the choice is cremation, the ashes may be buried in an urn at a cemetery, placed in a columbarium, or scattered at one or more locations.

Every state has regulations concerning the scattering of ashes, so check with your state agency that regulates burials. The scattering of ashes at sea must be done 3 nautical miles from land, and the Environmental Protection Agency needs notice within 30 days. You can file that notice online at www.epa.gov/reg3esd1/coast/burialform.htm.

Some people are considering natural or "green" burials. With a natural burial, the body would not be embalmed and would be promptly buried in the ground in a biodegradable coffin made of cardboard or bamboo, or in a shroud. Other possible elements of a green burial are having a tree or shrub planted instead of a stone grave marker and requesting that instead of bouquets of cut flowers, gifts be made to the favorite charity.

Those of the Jewish faith have special rituals for the washing of the body, staying with the body until burial, and prompt burial without embalming.

✓ Make the funeral arrangements

Depending on your loved one's family, cultural, or religious traditions, he or she may have decided that there should be no service or ceremony. Or, your loved one may prefer a lively gathering of family and friends to celebrate his or her life, a memorial service, a viewing at a mortuary, a wake, or a religious service in his or her place of worship. A funeral generally means that the body of the deceased is present, whereas a memorial service is held when the body is not present, has already been buried, or has been cremated.

You need to verify if your loved one had a preference for a funeral director and if any options have been preplanned or prepaid. Many funeral directors offer preneed contracts in which the person pays a fixed price for his or her funeral in the future. An advantage of prepaying includes fixing the costs at today's prices for the choice of a casket and other services that may cost more in the future. It's essential that you work with the funeral home that has the preneed contract so that you will know both the choices your loved one made and what has already been paid for. Funeral directors must give you written price lists that tell you the costs for body preparation and transportation, caskets or urns, and other goods and services.

If your loved one made prearrangements with a funeral home, you will be relieved of the stress of having to make many decisions about the preferred goods and services. If those plans were not made in advance of the death, you have a great number of options to consider.

A funeral director can assist you in carrying out the type of commemoration your loved one wanted. You'll need to determine the type of casket, if any, to use as well as other arrangements for any service or ceremony. Funeral directors can also help with arrangements for the grave marker or headstone. In the Jewish tradition, the family may wait for a year to unveil the headstone. You'll also need to determine the inscription for the headstone or grave marker. Headstones typically extend above the ground to identify the person buried. Grave markers lay flat on the ground. Some cemeteries or memorial parks require grave markers to make it easier to care for the grounds.

Other decisions you need to make include selecting the family members and friends who will participate in the service. Who will read selections of scripture, give the eulogy, or reflect on memories or experiences with the loved one? It's a good idea to make sure that those who will be speaking have copies of their remarks prepared and have practiced what they will say. It can be a very difficult responsibility to speak to the assembled family and friends at a time of grief. Don't be surprised if people are hesitant or decline to speak because they believe that they just can't control their emotions. Practicing and having an available supply of tissues may build their confidence that they can do it.

Will you select special music or musicians to enhance the service? Does your loved one's tradition call for pallbearers who carry or escort the casket from the service and to the gravesite? As you make these decisions, keep foremost in your mind what your loved one would want and how you can best honor and comply with his or her wishes.

✓ Research the cost of funerals

Each funeral option comes with a price tag. Funerals can cost thousands of dollars. You may wish to take the time to compare price lists at several different funeral homes. You can supply your own casket—you can even shop online for a casket—and the funeral home cannot charge you an extra fee if you don't purchase one through the funeral director. Resist any pressure to overspend what your family can afford out of a sense of obligation to honor your loved one in an extravagant way. It's smart to know what your state laws do or do not require, such as embalming the body. Costs can be saved by limiting the hours of visitation or providing a favorite outfit instead of costly burial clothing.

Along with making prior choices about the funeral, your loved one may have prepaid for those choices. If any of the costs have already been paid, you need to make sure that you have a copy of that contract before making any arrangements. You don't want to pay for funeral services only to find out later that the costs were already covered at a different funeral home. Check to see if the prices paid for the goods and services are guaranteed at the preset amount. Guaranteed prices are not required in most states. You need to make sure that you know what services will be covered, what has been paid for, and what extra amounts you will need.

Preneed funeral arrangement may be governed by special state laws, and in most states, funeral homes are regulated by licensing boards. State laws may require that any moneys entrusted to a funeral director be placed in some sort of interest-bearing account, funeral trust, or funeral insurance policies. A funeral trust allows preneed money to be pooled with other preneed funds and managed by a trustee other than the funeral director. Some funeral director associations act as trustees of the pooled funds. Funeral insurance policies are sold by a number of insurance companies. These policies can be used only to pay the costs of a funeral or burial. The face value of the policy is payable to the policy's beneficiary, who then is responsible for paying the funeral director. If you have any difficulties in getting the terms of a prepaid contract honored, contact the state board governing mortuary services.

You should also check to see if your loved one made any other provisions to cover the cost of funerals. One way is to set aside money in a pay on death (POD) account at a financial institution. With a POD account, a beneficiary is named; this person is entitled to the money only after the depositor has died and can use that money to pay for funeral and burial expenses. Another way is to have a life insurance policy specially designated to cover these expenses.

✓ Arrange for the burial

If the body is to be buried, you'll need to know if your loved one previously purchased a lot at a cemetery, wished to be buried in a family plot, or has a crypt in a mausoleum. If your loved one purchased a lot, you'll need to locate a copy of the burial plot deed. The sexton or other official at the cemetery may have a copy of the deed on file. Find out about any additional charges for opening and closing the grave site and for the perpetual care of the site. Some sites have restrictions on the days or times that graveside services can be held.

If there are no plans, you will need to make arrangements for where the body will be buried. If your loved one was a veteran, review the information in Chapter 4 on veterans' burial benefits, such as a burial plot in a national cemetery, a flag for the casket, or a grave marker.

✓ Notify friends and family of the death and funeral arrangements

The task of notifying friends and family may be something you will personally want to do, or you may ask others to share in this responsibility. Some may best be notified by phone call, whereas a letter, printed death notice, e-mail, or social media posting is an appropriate way to let others know of the death. Immediate family and employers should be told as soon as possible. You might wait until plans for the funeral and burial are settled to let others know. Consider if you wish to include any information about a favorite charity where donations could be made in memory of the deceased.

✓ Ensure the safety of the home and pets

It's important to make sure that your loved one's residence is secure. Unfortunately, thieves read obituaries and may exploit the opportunity to break into a home when they know that the owner has died. If the home is going to be vacant for any time period, ask the local police department to keep an eye on the house with drive-by patrols to check for anything suspicious. Make sure that papers and mail are collected daily so that the house doesn't appear vacated. You may want to set some lights on timers to go on and off in the evening so that the house looks occupied. Change the locks if you are not certain who has extra keys.

You'll need to make immediate arrangements for the care of any pets, if your loved one hasn't already let his or her wishes be known. Pet care might be a good task to delegate to a friend or neighbor who has volunteered to help. The teenage neighbor can make sure that the pets have food and water, are walked, or have clean litter boxes. If necessary, you may have to board the pet temporarily at a kennel until a permanent new home can be found.

✓ Maintain lists of helpers and help needed

You will want to have at least two lists. One list should be an ongoing record of people who have called on you, sent flowers, mailed sympathy cards, made donations to charities, or offered other expressions of sympathy. Place all the cards (and envelopes) or e-mails in a folder so that you'll have them available to reread later for warm memories. This list will come in useful when you have a chance to acknowledge everyone's kindness with a thank-you note.

The other list contains things other people can do for you. You might jot down tasks as they come to you so that when people ask what they can do to help, you'll have suggestions already in mind. The list could have such items as walk the dog, go to the post office, stop at the grocery store or dry cleaners, telephone friends, or mow the grass. Use the assigned tasks checklist on page 75 to keep track of who is doing what.

✓ Arrange for a visual tribute

You and your family may want to create a visual tribute to your loved one. It may be as simple as making sure that a good photograph of your loved one is displayed at the viewing or funeral. You may also want to find a photo to include with the obituary. Consider whether you want to create a scrapbook of photos that portray important events and people in your loved one's life. A grouping of framed photos and special mementos is another idea. With the growing popularity and convenience of digital photography, some families create a slide show of photos that is shown as part of the service. Check with the funeral home or place where you are holding a ceremony to see if it has software that you can use to develop the visual tribute. Your loved one's favorite music may accompany the collage of slides.

✓ Write and submit the obituary

Writing an obituary can be a daunting task. At the most basic level, it is a notice in a newspaper of a death and an announcement of funeral arrangements, but it can be so much more. Think more about writing about the person's life than his or her death. It can be a chance to celebrate and honor a cherished life story. Think about how your loved one would want to be remembered. Pulling together interesting details about the person's life can help those in the family and in the community know more about one of their members.

An obituary is also a record of family history for future generations. You'll want to strike a balance of how many generations and family relations you want to mention. Some family trees can get rather complicated with many branches. Check and recheck that you mention the family members with the correct relationship. You don't want to mistakenly leave out a sibling, confuse a nephew with a grandson, or write that a family member is deceased when that person is alive and well.

You should aim to make it accurate, complete, and lively so that friends reading will say, "That's just who she was," and all readers will say, "I wish I knew her." An accurate obituary has the correct dates of birth, marriage, and death. All names of places and family should be spelled correctly. Proofread it, ask someone else to read it for accuracy, and put it aside until tomorrow to read it with a fresh eye.

The obituary should give the time and place of the funeral or memorial service so that friends and community members will know when the services will be held. If those arrangements aren't yet in place, you can suggest contacting the funeral home for the details.

Also mention where memorial donations could be sent, if you prefer that people not send flowers. Remember that it is your loved one's choice of charities, not yours.

Most newspapers have a word limit for obituaries, perhaps 150 words. Others charge a fee for anything longer than a brief death notice and funeral arrangements. Most papers charge by inches of column space, so a lengthy obituary can cost a few hundred dollars. The funeral director can give you guidance on what the local newspapers expect and accept. A basic obituary may be part of the funeral package, so ask what additional inches of type will cost. Also ask if there is template or sample you can follow. Pick up a copy of the newspapers in which the obituary will appear so that you can get an idea of the preferred format. Check with the funeral home or the newspaper directly to find out the deadline for receiving copy for the next day's edition and how you should submit the copy. Most likely the paper will want you to e-mail an electronic copy.

✓ Locate and share legacy information such as an ethical will

Ethical wills may be one of the most cherished and meaningful gifts for a family. In an ethical will, individuals can share their values, blessings, life's lessons, hopes and dreams for the future, and love and forgiveness for family, friends, and future generations. An ethical will is an opportunity to put down on paper memories, insights, and special wisdom that shouldn't be lost or forgotten.

Ethical wills are not new. They are an ancient tradition for passing on personal values, beliefs, blessings, and advice to future generations. Initially, ethical wills were transmitted orally. Over time, they evolved into written documents. Today, ethical wills can be recorded on video as a cherished legacy for later generations. Ethical wills are not considered legal documents, in contrast to a living will with medical treatment preferences or a last will and testament that distributes property.

Be on the lookout for an ethical will as you go through papers or electronic files. It might be in the safe-deposit box, with an attorney, or with a religious leader. You'll want to follow any directions in the ethical will as to the timing or occasion when it is to be shared with family members.

First Things Action Checklists

Burial

❑ I have arranged for a burial.

❑ I do not need to arrange for a burial.

❑ I have identified the cemetery lot.

❑ I do not need to arrange for a cemetery lot.

The ownership of the lot is in the name of: _____

The lot is located at:

Cemetery: _____

Section: _____ Lot: _____

Address: _____

_____

Contact person at cemetery:

Name: _____

Phone number: _____

Location of deed: _____

❑ I have arranged for a grave marker.

❑ I have arranged for a headstone.

❑ I will arrange for a grave marker or headstone at a later date.

❑ I have contacted the Department of Veterans Affairs to arrange for a veteran's grave marker.

❑ I have contacted the Department of Veterans Affairs to arrange for a veteran's service medallion.

The following words should be placed on the grave marker or headstone:

_____

_____

_____

_____

Celebration of Life

❏   I have arranged a celebration of life ceremony.

❏   I do not need to arrange a celebration of life ceremony.

Type of celebration: _____

Arrangement details:

Place: _____

Time: _____

People to invite:

_____

_____

_____

_____

_____

_____

_____

_____

_____

_____

Food and beverage to be served:

_____

_____

_____

_____

❏   I have created music for the celebration.

❏   I have created a video or slide show for the celebration.

❏   I have created other special tributes for the celebration.

People who will help with the arrangements:

Who: _____ What: _____

Who: _____ What: _____

Who: _____ What: _____

Who: _____ What: _____

Who: _____ What: _____

Charities

❑ There will be no specific entities to receive memorial donations or gifts to charities.

❑ My loved one or I have selected the following entities to receive memorial donations or gifts to charities.

Charity name: _____

Charity address where donations should be sent: _____

_____

Contact person: _____

Connection with the deceased: _____

Charity name: _____

Charity address where donations should be sent: _____

_____

Contact person: _____

Connection with the deceased: _____

Charity name: _____

Charity address where donations should be sent: _____

_____

Contact person: _____

Connection with the deceased: _____

Charity name: _____

Charity address where donations should be sent: _____

_____

Contact person: _____

Connection with the deceased: _____

Cremation

❑   I have arranged for the body to be cremated.

❑   I do not need to arrange for the body to be cremated.

Crematorium: _____

Address: _____

_____

Phone: _____ Website: _____

Following the cremation, the ashes will be disbursed as follows:

❑   To be scattered: _____

❑   To be placed in an urn and buried or entombed: _____

❑   Other: _____

❑   I have notified the Environmental Protection Agency that the ashes were scattered at sea or in a lake.

Donation of Organs and Tissues

- ❏ My loved one consented to donate organs or tissues.
- ❏ I have checked the state's organ donation registry.
- ❏ I have consented to the donation of the following organs or tissues:

Organs:

- ❏ Heart
- ❏ Kidneys
- ❏ Liver
- ❏ Lungs
- ❏ Pancreas
- ❏ Other _____

Tissues:

- ❏ Blood vessels
- ❏ Bone
- ❏ Cartilage
- ❏ Corneas
- ❏ Heart valves
- ❏ Inner ear
- ❏ Intestines
- ❏ Skin
- ❏ Other _____

Organ procurement organization:

Contact person: _____

Telephone number: _____

Entombment

❑   I have arranged for the entombment of the body.

❑   I do not need to arrange for an entombment.

The ownership of the crypt is in the name of: _____

The mausoleum is located at:

Cemetery: _____

Section: _____ Crypt: _____

Address: _____

_____

Other description: _____

_____

Location of deed: _____

❑   I have arranged for a crypt marker.

The following words are to be placed on it:

_____

_____

_____

_____

Ethical Will/Legacy Documents

❑   I have located an ethical will.

❑   I have located other legacy documents.

❑   I have made arrangements to distribute these legacy documents as follows:

_____

_____

_____

_____

Funeral or Memorial Service Arrangements

❑ I have arranged a funeral.

❑ I have arranged a memorial service.

❑ I do not need to arrange a funeral or memorial service.

The service will be for:

❑ Friends and relatives

❑ Private

❑ Other: _____

The body:

❑ Will be present

❑ Will not be present

The casket will be:

❑ Closed

❑ Open

❑ The deceased will wear: _____

The following hymns, poems, and music will be used during the service:

_____

_____

_____

_____

The following flowers will be used for the service:

_____

_____

_____

_____

❑ I have requested that no floral arrangements be used for the service.

After the service, the floral arrangements will be distributed as follows:

- ❑ Nursing home
- ❑ Hospital
- ❑ Senior center
- ❑ Other: _____

I have arranged for the following visual tribute:

_____

_____

_____

_____

The following people will assist in the preparation of the visual tribute:

_____

_____

_____

_____

The following people will participate in the service:

- ❑ Service leader: _____
- ❑ Eulogy: _____
- ❑ Personal reflections: _____
- ❑ Readings: _____
- ❑ Musicians: _____
- ❑ Pallbearers: _____

_____

_____

- ❑ Other participants: _____

_____

_____

I have made these other arrangements:

_____

_____

_____

_____

Funeral Expenses

❑ I have located the following funeral prearrangements.

❑ I have located the preneed contract.

Funeral home: _____

Funeral director: _____

Address: _____

_____

Phone: _____

The preneed contract is located: _____

The preneed contract guarantees the price of stated goods and services:

❑ Yes

❑ No

The following funeral services have been prepaid:

❑ Basic professional services

❑ Casket

❑ Alternative container

❑ Urn for cremains

❑ Body preparation

❑ Embalming

❑ Public or family viewing or visitation

❑ Service at the mortuary

❑ Crematory fee

❑ Transportation of the body

❑ Graveside service

❑ Obituary preparation

❑ Copies of death certificate

❑ Burial clothing

❑ Recording of service

❑ Preparation of photo DVD or CD

❑ Memorial book

❑ Memorial folders or service bulletin

❑ Limousine for family members

❑ Outer burial vault or grave liner

❑ I have received price lists for all funeral goods and services to be provided by the funeral home.

❑ I have located the following pay on death (POD) account to be used to pay for funeral expenses:

Account #: _____

Amount in the account: _____

Financial institution: _____

❑ I have located the following pooled funeral trust or funeral insurance policy:

Account/policy #: _____

Amount in the trust or policy: _____

Insurance company: _____

Contact information: _____

Obituary

❏   No obituary will be prepared.

❏   I have prepared an obituary.

The following information should be included in the obituary:

_____

_____

_____

_____

_____

_____

_____

_____

The following people will help prepare the obituary:

_____

_____

_____

❏   A photo will be included with the obituary.

The following people will proofread the obituary:

_____

_____

The obituary will appear in the following newspapers:

_____

_____

The deadline for obituary copy is: _____

The cost for running the obituary is: _____

Electronic copy of the obituary should be sent to: _____

_____

Persons to Contact

The following persons should be contacted to let them know of the death:

Name: _____

Relationship: _____

Phone: _____ E-mail: _____

Address: _____

_____

Name: _____

Relationship: _____

Phone: _____ E-mail: _____

Address: _____

_____

Name: _____

Relationship: _____

Phone: _____ E-mail: _____

Address: _____

_____

Name: _____

Relationship: _____

Phone: _____ E-mail: _____

Address: _____

_____

Name: _____

Relationship: _____

Phone: _____ E-mail: _____

Address: _____

_____

Name: _____

Relationship: _____

Phone: _____ E-mail: _____

Address: _____

_____

Name: _____

Relationship: _____

Phone: _____ E-mail: _____

Address: _____

_____

Name: _____

Relationship: _____

Phone: _____ E-mail: _____

Address: _____

_____

Name: _____

Relationship: _____

Phone: _____ E-mail: _____

Address: _____

_____

Name: _____

Relationship: _____

Phone: _____ E-mail: _____

Address: _____

_____

Name: _____

Relationship: _____

Phone: _____ E-mail: _____

Address: _____

_____

Name: _____

Relationship: _____

Phone: _____ E-mail: _____

Address: _____

_____

Pet Care

- ❑ There are no pets needing care.
- ❑ My loved one has made the following arrangements for the care of the pets.
- ❑ I have made the following arrangements for the care of the pets.
- ❑ I have made financial arrangements for the care of the pets.

The following are the arrangements for the care of the pets:

_____

_____

_____

_____

_____

_____

_____

The following are the financial arrangements for the care of the pets:

_____

_____

_____

_____

_____

_____

Whole Body Donation

❑ My loved one did not make prearrangements for whole body donation.

❑ I have identified the following prearrangements for whole body donation made with the following medical school or research organization:

Medical school: _____

Address: _____

_____

Phone: _____

Contact person: _____

Research organization: _____

Address: _____

_____

Phone: _____

Contact person: _____

First Things: Other

Other miscellaneous information of interest:

_____

_____

_____

_____

_____

_____

_____

_____

_____

_____

_____

_____

_____

_____

_____

_____

_____

_____

_____

_____

_____

_____

_____

_____

_____

_____

_____

_____

_____

_____

_____

_____

_____

_____

CHAPTER 2

GET ORGANIZED FOR WHAT COMES NEXT

The hours, weeks, and months after a death can be difficult times for all members of the family. On top of dealing with the loss of a loved one, there can be myriad details to take care of. Managing grief while making sure that bills are paid on time, cleaning out a house or apartment, sending copies of the death certification to all the right places, and getting ready to settle the estate can be overwhelming. All the checklists in this book can help you get organized so that you know what needs to be done, how to do it, and who can help you.

In this chapter, you'll find suggestions for ways you can get organized to tackle what lies ahead. Perhaps the first step in figuring out what you do know is to make an initial pass through the checklists and check off what you do know or information readily at hand. You may be pleasantly surprised to realize that you already know the basics about the details and decisions.

Your loved one may have let you know about his or her wishes for a memorial service, prepared a letter of instruction, made lists of passwords, created an estate plan with a will and/or a trust, and organized files of financial documents. To make matters even easier for you, he or she may have filled out the checklists in my first book, *The ABA Checklist for Family Heirs*. If so, count your blessings that much of the detective work has been done for you.

Then mark off the items on the checklist that you know you don't need to know. Depending on your loved one's circumstances, you may be able to quickly dispatch pages of checklists. For example, if your loved one was not a veteran (or married to a veteran), skip over the entire section about the Veterans Administration. If you are sure there's never been a pension fund, move on. No cars or driver's license? Then there's no need to go to the Department of Motor Vehicles.

My to-do checklist

Done   **Need to Do**

Done	Need to Do	
❏	❏	Set up a filing system
❏	❏	Make copies of all documents
❏	❏	Keep notes of conversations
❏	❏	Track down family history
❏	❏	Complete the checklists for Chapter 2

Get organized action checklists

The Action Checklists in Chapter 2 are set out in the following order:

- *Personal History of the Deceased*
- *Children and Grandchildren*
- *Parents*
- *Brothers and Sisters*
- *Grandparents*
- *Stepgrandparents*
- *Aunts, Uncles, and Cousins*
- *Stepparents*
- *Stepbrothers and Stepsisters*
- *Records to Locate*
- *Get Organized: Other*

✓ Set up a filing system

One glance at the checklist of records to locate in this chapter should tell you that you've got to have a system to organize all this information. It may even take several systems! Some are paper files, others will be stored electronically in a computer folder. Keys, rare books, artworks, and personal possessions can't be neatly stored in a file folder. Pieces of plastic such as credit cards, ATM cards, organ donor cards, driver's licenses, Medicare cards, and Social Security cards need a safe and secure place.

You'll need ways to keep track of what you have and where it is so that you can find any bit of information when you need it. Use the records checklist to indicate not only what you have found and what you need to find, but also where you have it stored. Is it in the safe deposit box or a file folder? If it is an electronic file, what's the folder name?

Now is the time to invest in storage containers and a box of file folders. You will be collecting lots of papers and documents. Each document should go in its own folder with a clear label that identifies the document. This step will save much time later on when you need to find a specific document. You may want to invest in a document scanner or printer with a scanner so that you can create electronic files of important papers. While you are at the office supply store, pick up a paper shredder so that you can safely dispose of papers you don't need.

Electronic files on your computer likewise need to be clearly named and sorted into folders and subfolders. Set up a special folder or folders where you keep all related e-mails, too. Use your calendaring function on your computer to track deadlines and due dates.

One of the first folders that you want to establish contains the cards and messages the family receives as expressions of condolences. In this folder, you collect cards with envelopes and e-mails, a list of who sent flowers, notes on who helped the family with meals or errands, and letters from charities acknowledging donations in your loved one's memory. Keep the envelopes so that you'll have the addresses at hand when you later send thank-you notes.

Use the assigned tasks checklist in Chapter 3 to keep track of who is taking on the responsibility to help you gather information and documents.

✓ Make copies of all documents

The importance of making copies can't be stressed enough. Copy all originals before you share them with anyone. You've worked hard to gather this information, so don't let any original documents leave your possession. Make copies of all correspondence and the documents you enclosed. If a letter and attachments get lost in the mail, you want to have copies of everything you sent. Keep electronic copies of e-mails sent and received. If someone wants an original, make sure that they make a copy and return the original to you before you leave their presence.

Get at least twelve copies of the death certificate. The funeral director should be able to give you multiple copies and get you more when you run out of copies. As you'll see throughout this book, many places are going to want to have the death certificate. Have a file folder just for the death certificates so that you can make sure you know where they are.

✓ Keep notes of conversations

Put a notebook next to your phone so that you can keep track of conversations. You want to take notes of whom you spoke with (first and last name with contact number including extension), key points of the conversation, and the date and time of the call. This information is especially important when talking with government agencies or financial institutions. When you have to follow up on a call, it is useful to be able to say, "Your agent Benjamin Whitson told me on July 6th that I could expect an answer to my question by August 1st."

✓ Track down family history

There are two reasons you need to organize information about your loved one's family history. First, you will want to include information about his or her closest family members in the obituary. Although you may not be able to collect all the information listed in the family

33

Caution: Know to whom you are giving information. When you make the contact, appointment, or phone call, it's okay to give out necessary information about your loved one. Be careful, however, about what personal information about your loved one you share. If people contact you asking for personal details, such as bank account numbers, Social Security number, or date of death or birth, reply only if you know exactly whom they are and why they need the information. The caller may be fishing for information to steal your loved one's identity.

Independently verify what the contacting party says and why he or she is contacting you. You can do so by first asking "who, what, and why." If it is a phone call, hang up. You or a friend or relative should then check the contact's phone number, website, or e-mail address through an independent source. Search the name on the Internet, check the phone book for the number, or call your state attorney general to verify the information that you were given.

---

history checklists in the few days after a death, use the checklists to make sure that you haven't left anyone out of the family tree who should be mentioned in the obituary. Later, you may want to go back to filling in missing information about the relatives. When the family is gathered for the funeral, you may want to take the opportunity to add any missing details, check the spelling of names, and figure out if Margaret is a cousin or a niece.

The second reason you need this information is to determine possible heirs. During the probate process, relatives or "next of kin" need to be notified of the probate of the will. Names and addresses of all the family members who are entitled to notice will need to be gathered. If there is no will, all the family relationships will need to be properly established. Whether someone will inherit any property from the deceased will depend on the precise degree of relationship and whether there are any others with that same relationship. For example, in most states, if there were two sons and one daughter each with one child but the daughter had previously died, the two surviving sons would each take a third and the surviving child of the daughter would take a third. Refer to Chapter 11 on probate for more information on how property is distributed when there is no will.

Get Organized Action Checklists

Personal History of the Deceased

Name:

_____

          First   *Middle*   *Last*

Name at birth:

_____

          First   *Middle*   *Last*

Place of birth:

_____

          City   *State*   *Country*

Date of birth: _____

Legal name change:

_____

          First   *Middle*   *Last*

Legal name change date: _____

Legal name change court:

_____

          Court   *City*   *State*

Citizenship: _____

- ❏ By birth
- ❏ By naturalization

Naturalization date: _____

Naturalization place:

_____

| | City | State | Country |

Military veteran:

- ❏ Yes
- ❏ No

Branch of service: _____

Dates of service: _____

Serial number: _____ Rank: _____

Type of discharge: _____

****

Social Security number: _____

****

Passport number: _____ Expiration: _____

Country of issue: _____

****

Driver's license number: _____ Expiration: _____

State of issue: _____

****

Marital status:

- ❏ Divorced
- ❏ Married
- ❏ Never married
- ❏ Widowed

First Spouse

Name of spouse at birth: _____

Date of birth: _____

Place of birth: _____

Date of marriage: _____

Date of divorce: _____

Date of death: _____

Spouse is buried at: _____

Cause of death: _____

Name at present: _____

Phone: _____ Fax: _____

Address: _____

_____

Second Spouse

Name of spouse at birth: _____

Date of birth: _____

Place of birth: _____

Date of marriage: _____

Date of divorce: _____

Date of death: _____

Spouse is buried at: _____

Cause of death: _____

Name at present: _____

Phone: _____ Fax: _____

Address: _____

_____

Third Spouse

Name of spouse at birth: _____

Date of birth: _____

Place of birth: _____

Date of marriage: _____

Date of divorce: _____

Date of death: _____

Spouse is buried at: _____

Cause of death: _____

Name at present: _____

Phone: _____ Fax: _____

Address: _____

_____

Children and Grandchildren

Name at present: _____

Phone: _____ Fax: _____

Address: _____

_____

E-mail: _____

Name at birth: _____

Place of birth:

_____

City   *County*   *State*   *Country*

Child is buried at: _____

Cause of death: _____

❑ Child has never been married.

❑ Child is currently married.

❑ Child has been married _____ times.

Child	Name of Spouse	Date of Marriage	Date of Divorce	Date of Death
#1				
#2				
#3				

❑ Child has not had any children.

❑ Child has _____ children.

❑ Child has _____ adopted children.

❑ Child has _____ born children.

Grandchild	Name of Child at Birth	Current Name of Child	Date of Birth	Date of Death
#1				
#2				
#3				
#4				
#5				
#6				

*****

Name at present: _____

Phone: _____ Fax: _____

Address: _____

_____

E-mail: _____

Name at birth: _____

Place of birth:

_____

      City   *County*   *State*   *Country*

Child is buried at: _____

Cause of death: _____

❑   Child has never been married.

❑   Child is currently married.

❑   Child has been married _____ times.

Child	Name of Spouse	Date of Marriage	Date of Divorce	Date of Death
#1				
#2				
#3				

❑ Child has not had any children.

❑ Child has _____ children.

❑ Child has _____ adopted children.

❑ Child has _____ born children.

Grandchild	Name of Child at Birth	Current Name of Child	Date of Birth	Date of Death
#1				
#2				
#3				
#4				
#5				
#6				

*****

Name at present: _____

Phone: _____ Fax: _____

Address: _____

_____

E-mail: _____

Name at birth: _____

Place of birth:

_____

    City   *County*   *State*   *Country*

Child is buried at: _____

Cause of death: _____

❑ Child has never been married.

❑ Child is currently married.

❑ Child has been married _____ times.

Child	Name of Spouse	Date of Marriage	Date of Divorce	Date of Death
#1				
#2				
#3				

❑ Child has not had any children.

❑ Child has _____ children.

❑ Child has _____ adopted children.

❑ Child has _____ born children.

Grandchild	Name of Child at Birth	Current Name of Child	Date of Birth	Date of Death
#1				
#2				
#3				
#4				
#5				
#6				

*****

Name at present: _____

Phone: _____ Fax: _____

Address: _____

_____

E-mail: _____

Name at birth: _____

Place of birth:

_____

    City   *County*   *State*   *Country*

Child is buried at: _____

Cause of death: _____

❑   Child has never been married.

❑   Child is currently married.

❑   Child has been married _____ times.

Child	Name of Spouse	Date of Marriage	Date of Divorce	Date of Death
#1				
#2				
#3				

❑   Child has not had any children.

❑   Child has _____ children.

❑   Child has _____ adopted children.

❑   Child has _____ born children.

Grandchild	Name of Child at Birth	Current Name of Child	Date of Birth	Date of Death
#1				
#2				
#3				
#4				
#5				
#6				

Parents

Name of father: _____

Phone: _____ Fax: _____

Address: _____

_____

E-mail: _____

Date of birth: _____ Place of birth: _____

Date of death: _____ Cause of death: _____

Name of mother: _____

Relationship: _____

Phone: _____ Fax: _____

Address: _____

_____

E-mail: _____

Date of birth: _____ Place of birth: _____

Date of death: _____ Cause of death: _____

Brothers and Sisters

Name at present: _____

Phone: _____ Fax: _____

Address: _____

_____

E-mail: _____

Date of birth: _____

Place of birth:

_____

| | | | |
| *City* | *County* | *State* | *Country* |

Date of death: _____ Cause of death: _____

Sibling is buried at: _____

❑ Sibling has never been married.

❑ Sibling is currently married.

❑ Sibling has been married _____ times.

Sibling	Name of Spouse	Date of Marriage	Date of Divorce	Date of Death
#1				
#2				
#3				

❑ Sibling has not had any children.

❑ Sibling has _____ children.

❑ Sibling has _____ adopted children.

❑ Sibling has _____ born children.

Child	Name of Child at Birth	Current Name of Child	Date of Birth	Date of Death
#1				
#2				
#3				
#4				
#5				
#6				

*****

Name at present: _____

Phone: _____ Fax: _____

Address: _____

_____

E-mail: _____

Date of birth: _____

Place of birth:

_____

| *City* | *County* | *State* | *Country* |

Date of death: _____ Cause of death: _____

Sibling is buried at: _____

❑   Sibling has never been married.

❑   Sibling is currently married.

❑   Sibling has been married _____ times.

Sibling	Name of Spouse	Date of Marriage	Date of Divorce	Date of Death
#1				
#2				
#3				

❑   Sibling has not had any children.

❑   Sibling has _____ children.

❑ Sibling has _____ adopted children.

❑ Sibling has _____ born children.

Child	Name of Child at Birth	Current Name of Child	Date of Birth	Date of Death
#1				
#2				
#3				
#4				
#5				
#6				

*****

Name at present: _____

Phone: _____ Fax: _____

Address: _____

_____

E-mail: _____

Date of birth: _____

Place of birth:

_____

     City   *County*   *State*   *Country*

Date of death: _____ Cause of death: _____

Sibling is buried at: _____

❑ Sibling has never been married.

❑ Sibling is currently married.

❑ Sibling has been married _____ times.

Sibling	Name of Spouse	Date of Marriage	Date of Divorce	Date of Death
#1				
#2				
#3				

- ❑ Sibling has not had any children.
- ❑ Sibling has _____ children.
- ❑ Sibling has _____ adopted children.
- ❑ Sibling has _____ born children.

Child	Name of Child at Birth	Current Name of Child	Date of Birth	Date of Death
#1				
#2				
#3				
#4				
#5				
#6				

*****

Name at present: _____

Phone: _____ Fax: _____

Address: _____

_____

E-mail: _____

Date of birth: _____

Place of birth:

_____

City	*County*	*State*	*Country*

Date of death: _____ Cause of death: _____

Sibling is buried at: _____

- ❑ Sibling has never been married.
- ❑ Sibling is currently married.
- ❑ Sibling has been married _____ times.

Sibling	Name of Spouse	Date of Marriage	Date of Divorce	Date of Death
#1				
#2				
#3				

❑   Sibling has not had any children.

❑   Sibling has _____ children.

❑   Sibling has _____ adopted children.

❑   Sibling has _____ born children.

Child	Name of Child at Birth	Current Name of Child	Date of Birth	Date of Death
#1				
#2				
#3				
#4				
#5				
#6				

*****

Name at present: _____

Phone: _____ Fax: _____

Address: _____

_____

E-mail: _____

Date of birth: _____

Place of birth:

_____

   City   *County*   *State*   *Country*

Date of death: _____ Cause of death: _____

Sibling is buried at: _____

❑ Sibling has never been married.

❑ Sibling is currently married.

❑ Sibling has been married _____ times.

Sibling	Name of Spouse	Date of Marriage	Date of Divorce	Date of Death
#1				
#2				
#3				

❑ Sibling has not had any children.

❑ Sibling has _____ children.

❑ Sibling has _____ adopted children.

❑ Sibling has _____ born children.

Child	Name of Child at Birth	Current Name of Child	Date of Birth	Date of Death
#1				
#2				
#3				
#4				
#5				
#6				

*****

Name at present: _____

Phone: _____ Fax: _____

Address: _____

_____

E-mail: _____

Date of birth: _____

Place of birth:

_____

| *City* | *County* | *State* | *Country* |

Date of death: _____ Cause of death: _____

Sibling is buried at: _____

- ❑ Sibling has never been married.
- ❑ Sibling is currently married.
- ❑ Sibling has been married _____ times.

Sibling	Name of Spouse	Date of Marriage	Date of Divorce	Date of Death
#1				
#2				
#3				

- ❑ Sibling has not had any children.
- ❑ Sibling has _____ children.
- ❑ Sibling has _____ adopted children.
- ❑ Sibling has _____ born children.

Child	Name of Child at Birth	Current Name of Child	Date of Birth	Date of Death
#1				
#2				
#3				
#4				
#5				
#6				

Grandparents

Name: _____

Relationship: _____

Phone: _____ Fax: _____

Address: _____

_____

E-mail: _____

Date of birth: _____ Place of birth: _____

Date of death: _____ Cause of death: _____

*****

Name: _____

Relationship: _____

Phone: _____ Fax: _____

Address: _____

_____

E-mail: _____

Date of birth: _____ Place of birth: _____

Date of death: _____ Cause of death: _____

*****

Name: _____

Relationship: _____

Phone: _____ Fax: _____

Address: _____

_____

E-mail: _____

Date of birth: _____ Place of birth: _____

Date of death: _____ Cause of death: _____

*****

Name: _____

Relationship: _____

Phone: _____ Fax: _____

Address: _____

_____

E-mail: _____

Date of birth: _____ Place of birth: _____

Date of death: _____ Cause of death: _____

Stepgrandparents

Name: _____

Relationship: _____

Phone: _____ Fax: _____

Address: _____

_____

E-mail: _____

Date of birth: _____ Place of birth: _____

Date of death: _____ Cause of death: _____

Name: _____

Relationship: _____

Phone: _____ Fax: _____

Address: _____

_____

E-mail: _____

Date of birth: _____ Place of birth: _____

Date of death: _____ Cause of death: _____

Aunts, Uncles, and Cousins

Name: _____

Relationship: _____

Phone: _____ Fax: _____

Address: _____

_____

E-mail: _____

Date of birth: _____ Place of birth: _____

Date of death: _____ Cause of death: _____

Name: _____

Relationship: _____

Phone: _____ Fax: _____

Address: _____

_____

E-mail: _____

Date of birth: _____ Place of birth: _____

Date of death: _____ Cause of death: _____

Name: _____

Relationship: _____

Phone: _____ Fax: _____

Address: _____

_____

E-mail: _____

Date of birth: _____ Place of birth: _____

Date of death: _____ Cause of death: _____

Name: _____

Relationship: _____

Phone: _____ Fax: _____

Address: _____

_____

E-mail: _____

Date of birth: _____ Place of birth: _____

Date of death: _____ Cause of death: _____

Name: _____

Relationship: _____

Phone: _____ Fax: _____

Address: _____

_____

E-mail: _____

Date of birth: _____ Place of birth: _____

Date of death: _____ Cause of death: _____

Name: _____

Relationship: _____

Phone: _____ Fax: _____

Address: _____

_____

E-mail: _____

Date of birth: _____ Place of birth: _____

Date of death: _____ Cause of death: _____

Name: _____

Relationship: _____

Phone: _____ Fax: _____

Address: _____

_____

E-mail: _____

Date of birth: _____ Place of birth: _____

Date of death: _____ Cause of death: _____

Name: _____

Relationship: _____

Phone: _____ Fax: _____

Address: _____

_____

E-mail: _____

Date of birth: _____ Place of birth: _____

Date of death: _____ Cause of death: _____

Stepparents

Name: _____

Relationship: _____

Phone: _____ Fax: _____

Address: _____

_____

E-mail: _____

Date of birth: _____ Place of birth: _____

Date of death: _____ Cause of death: _____

Name: _____

Relationship: _____

Phone: _____ Fax: _____

Address: _____

_____

E-mail: _____

Date of birth: _____ Place of birth: _____

Date of death: _____ Cause of death: _____

Stepbrothers and Stepsisters

Name: _____

Relationship: _____

Phone: _____ Fax: _____

Address: _____

_____

E-mail: _____

Date of birth: _____ Place of birth: _____

Date of death: _____ Cause of death: _____

Name: _____

Relationship: _____

Phone: _____ Fax: _____

Address: _____

_____

E-mail: _____

Date of birth: _____ Place of birth: _____

Date of death: _____ Cause of death: _____

Name: _____

Relationship: _____

Phone: _____ Fax: _____

Address: _____

_____

E-mail: _____

Date of birth: _____ Place of birth: _____

Date of death: _____ Cause of death: _____

Name: _____

Relationship: _____

Phone: _____ Fax: _____

Address: _____

_____

E-mail: _____

Date of birth: _____ Place of birth: _____

Date of death: _____ Cause of death: _____

Records to Locate

Record Type   **Location**

Personal History

- Adoption papers   _____
- Animal care information   _____
- Annulment decrees or judgments   _____
- Appointment book or calendar   _____
- Athletic awards   _____
- Award certificates   _____
- Birth certificates   _____
- Change of name certificates   _____
- Child care information   _____
- Civic awards   _____
- Divorce decrees or judgments   _____
- Dramatic awards   _____
- Driver's license   _____
- Educational awards   _____
- Educational certificates   _____
- Educational transcripts   _____
- Employment awards   _____
- Keys to residence   _____
- Keys to post office box   _____
- Keys to safe deposit box   _____
- Keys to vehicles   _____
- Keys to other real estate   _____
- Lock combinations   _____
- Membership awards   _____
- Membership certificates   _____
- Military awards   _____

❑ Military separation papers   _____

❑ Music/CDs catalog   _____

❑ Naturalization papers   _____

❑ Other awards   _____

❑ Passport   _____

❑ Passwords   _____

❑ Photo albums   _____

❑ Photos   _____

❑ Property care information   _____

❑ Security system information   _____

❑ Tax returns and records   _____

❑ Time-share records   _____

❑ Videos/movies catalog   _____

❑ Other   _____

❑ Other   _____

❑ Other   _____

Family History

❑ Adoption papers   _____

❑ Birth certificates   _____

❑ Family tree   _____

❑ Marriage certificates   _____

❑ Newspaper articles   _____

❑ Photo albums   _____

❑ Portraits   _____

❑ Other   _____

❑ Other   _____

❑ Other   _____

Insurance Policies

- ❑ Automobile   _____
- ❑ Life insurance   _____
- ❑ Long-term care   _____
- ❑ Medical   _____
- ❑ Medicare card   _____
- ❑ Medicare Part D   _____
- ❑ Residential   _____
- ❑ Umbrella   _____
- ❑ Other insurance   _____
- ❑ Other insurance   _____
- ❑ Other insurance   _____

Benefits

- ❑ 401(k) agreements   _____
- ❑ 403(b) agreements   _____
- ❑ Disability agreements   _____
- ❑ IRA agreements   _____
- ❑ Keogh plan agreements   _____
- ❑ Military separation papers   _____
- ❑ Pension agreements   _____
- ❑ SEP agreements   _____
- ❑ Social Security card   _____
- ❑ Social Security statement   _____
- ❑ Workers' compensation   _____
- ❑ Other   _____
- ❑ Other   _____
- ❑ Other   _____

Banking and Savings

❑ CD account statements   _____

❑ Checking account statements   _____

❑ Credit union account statements   _____

❑ Savings account statements   _____

❑ Savings bonds   _____

❑ Other   _____

❑ Other   _____

❑ Other   _____

Investments

❑ Brokerage account statements   _____

❑ Savings bonds   _____

❑ Other   _____

❑ Other   _____

❑ Other   _____

Real Estate

❑ Deeds   _____

❑ Home improvement records   _____

❑ Land contracts   _____

❑ Leases   _____

❑ Mortgages   _____

❑ Reverse mortgage   _____

❑ Tax records   _____

❑ Time-share agreements   _____

❑ Other   _____

❑ Other   _____

Other Assets and Debts

❑ Business records   _____

❑ Collectibles   _____

- ❑ Computers _____
- ❑ Copyrights _____
- ❑ Credit card contracts _____
- ❑ Jewelry appraisals _____
- ❑ Jewelry inventory _____
- ❑ Patents and trademarks _____
- ❑ Rare books _____
- ❑ Vehicles _____
- ❑ Vehicle certificates of title _____
- ❑ Warranties _____
- ❑ Websites _____
- ❑ Other _____
- ❑ Other _____

Estate Planning

- ❑ Trust agreement _____
- ❑ Will and codicils _____
- ❑ Other _____
- ❑ Other _____
- ❑ Other _____

Final Wishes

- ❑ Body bequeathal papers _____
- ❑ Celebration of life arrangements _____
- ❑ Cemetery deed _____
- ❑ Cremation arrangement _____
- ❑ Ethical will/legacy documents _____
- ❑ Preneed funeral contract _____
- ❑ Legacy information _____
- ❑ Letters to be sent _____
- ❑ Mausoleum deed _____

- ❑ People to contact _____
- ❑ Pet continuing care _____
- ❑ Uniform donor card _____
- ❑ Other _____
- ❑ Other _____

Get Organized: Other

Other miscellaneous information of interest:

_____

_____

_____

_____

_____

_____

_____

_____

_____

_____

_____

_____

_____

_____

_____

_____

_____

_____

_____

_____

_____

_____

_____

_____

_____

_____

_____

_____

_____

_____

_____

_____

_____

CHAPTER 3
BUILD A TEAM YOU CAN RELY ON

You are not in this situation alone. Just one glance at this book—with all the checklists of things you might need to do—and it's quite obvious that settling a loved one's affairs after death is not a one-person task. It's going to take a team and teamwork to handle all the details. You'll be able to ignore many of the things mentioned in the checklists in this book because they won't apply to you or your loved one. Although you'll want to handle some things yourself, many tasks can be delegated to others. Plus, you need to know what professional help is available. Which professional will you need to help you do what?

It's also going to take determining priorities of things you need to do sooner rather than later and identifying what can wait until a more appropriate time. Your personal circumstances and those of your deceased loved one are going to shape the priorities, the timing of what comes next, and who is going to be responsible for seeing that all the necessary decisions are made.

My to-do checklist

Done	Need to Do	
❑	❑	Know your family
❑	❑	Understand the stages of grief
❑	❑	Head off family discord
❑	❑	Draw on special talents
❑	❑	Identify the need for a lawyer
❑	❑	Find a financial advisor
❑	❑	Check on the background of any financial professional
❑	❑	Complete the checklists in Chapter 3

Build a team action checklists

The Action Checklists in Chapter 3 are set out in the following order:

- *Assigned Tasks*
- *Financial Professionals*
- *Lawyers*
- *Build a Team: Other*

✓ Know your family

You know your family best. As with most families, there will be relatives you can lean on for solid support. When they say they'll do something, you know it will be done correctly. You can count on them to accomplish the biggest or most difficult assignments. Others may be long on promises but a little short on follow-through. With some nudging or prompting on your part, they can be good helpers. Another member of the family may have a heart of gold but just not be able to manage the details. Some may be so emotional over the death that sound decisions cannot be expected at this time. Sometimes, unfortunately, other family members may seem to be at cross-purposes with any decision you are trying to make.

Depending on your role in the family, you may be the one to take the lead in making decisions about the funeral and then turn over the financial details to the executor or the trustee. As the surviving spouse, you may feel most comfortable relying on another family member or on a professional team. If you are reading this chapter because one of your parents has died, your place on the team may be to provide support as asked and be alert to ways to make sure things go smoothly. As the executor or trustee, you have many responsibilities ahead of you and many decisions to make, but you will still need open lines of communication among all the family members and a support team to get everything done.

✓ Understand the stages of grief

When dealing with difficult family members, it may be helpful to you if you understand that they may be at a different stage in the grief process. Elisabeth Kübler-Ross and David Kessler have outlined stages of feelings that many people go through in the process of dealing with the loss of another. These stages are called denial, anger, bargaining, depression, and acceptance. You can learn more about recognizing your own grief process and that of others around you at http://grief.com/the-five-stages/.

✓ Head off family discord

You may need to employ various strategies to head off family discord. You may even try a couple of different tactics to find what will work best in your family. Keeping lines of communication open can be very effective for keeping the peace. At the same time, you don't want to become exhausted trying to keep everyone informed about every little detail or explaining every decision over and over. One idea to try is a family meeting to talk things through and establish boundaries and rules of communication. You may want to:

- Take turns speaking and let everyone speak (once).
- Agree that once a decision has been made, discussions on that point are closed.
- Appoint a spokesperson or spokespersons for various branches of the family.
- Create a system of communication—telephone tree, e-mail list, social media outlet—that sets up who is responsible for informing other members of the family.
- Ask a neutral, nonfamily member, such as a faith leader, to facilitate a family meeting.

✓ Draw on special talents

Not everyone around you has the same talents and skills. Sister Sue may have the best list of relatives and be the right person to make calls about the death and funeral arrangements. Nephew Nick, who spends hours on the Internet, can take over figuring out the online accounts issues. Rita has a knack for genealogy and can pull together family history for the obituary. She can then pass that information on to Maria, who's a good writer. Ask Tom to use his pickup truck on the days you are sorting through and cleaning out the house or apartment. The grandsons can be recruited to mow the grass, and Louise might be able to take in the cats. To share the responsibilities, you may wish to assign each of the checklists in this book to a different individual.

When people ask how they can help, don't be shy to take them up on their offer. With the checklists, you can pinpoint large or small steps they can take to help you get everything done. It's important to keep track of who is doing what so that things don't get overlooked, bypassed, or duplicated. If there are important deadlines, be sure that the person taking on that task knows when each has to be done. One checklist in this chapter helps you record who has agreed to do what and by when they need to do it.

✓ Identify the need for a lawyer

You may already have a family lawyer who is familiar with your family's affairs or drafted your loved one's will. If so, this lawyer may be one of the first professionals you call. However, keep in mind that just because a lawyer helped draft the will, or even has been safe-keeping the will, does not mean that you have to use that same lawyer to handle the estate. In many cases, that person may be the best and most obvious choice, but there is no obligation to continue to use the services of the same lawyer who drafted the will.

When thinking about hiring a lawyer for any type of legal service or advice, you have to answer two related questions: whom should you choose, and what do you want the lawyer to do? Of key importance is finding a lawyer who has experience in that area of the law and in proper jurisdiction. Cousin Tim who went to law school may not be the best choice if Tim does not have experience with probate matters. The experienced probate lawyer in Michigan may not be sufficiently familiar with Texas law to settle a Texas estate. You'll want to find a lawyer who is licensed to practice and concentrates a substantial part of her or his practice in the state where your loved one's estate will be settled.

Legal note on domicile: Most estates need to be settled or "go through probate" in the county in which the deceased was living or "domiciled" at the time of death. In today's mobile society, figuring out where someone was domiciled can be complicated. For example, if someone has been living in a nursing home for the past year, is that person domiciled in that county or in the county where he or she still owns a home? That is the type of legal question you'll have to ask your lawyer to answer.

A good way to find a lawyer is to ask friends and family who have recently settled an estate for their recommendations. Another way is to contact the local or state bar association's lawyer referral service. The American Bar Association has a directory of lawyer referral services available in each state at http://apps.americanbar.org/legalservices/lris /directory/home.html. You may also want to consult the list of elder law attorneys who are members of the National Academy of Elder Law Attorneys at www.naela.org or probate fellows who are members of the American College of Trust and Estate Counsel at http://www.actec.org/public/roster/FindFellow.asp.

You'll want to interview several attorneys to learn of their experience in handling probate matters, talk about what you think you want the lawyer to do for you, and find out how the lawyer will charge for his or her services. Before selecting any lawyer, you want to make sure that the chemistry is right for your relationship and that expectations are understood.

Lawyers charge for their services in a variety of ways. It might be an hourly rate, or it may be a set fee for providing specific services. Some attorneys ask for a lump-sum retainer before beginning any work. The attorney would then draw down disbursements from the retained amount at the hourly rate as work is accomplished. It may be that at first the lawyer cannot calculate the total fee until he or she has a better understanding of the problems that might develop. You should, however, expect to receive detailed and frequent statements of services so that you can keep tabs on what has been done and what is being charged.

It is essential that you and the lawyer have the same expectations about what services are to be provided. You may want the lawyer to walk you through the steps you need to take to handle most matters on your own but be available to call from time to time for guidance when you run into a question. On the other hand, you may want the lawyer to handle all details so that you don't have to worry about getting everything done. You will want to have a signed letter of engagement that sets out in some detail what the lawyer is going to do for you.

Keep in mind that most lawyers concentrate their practices in some specific areas. For example, tax attorneys concentrate their practices on complicated tax matters. They can assist with the preparation of tax returns and give advice on how to avoid unnecessary estate taxes. Enrolled agents, who must pass a comprehensive exam, are able to represent you before the Internal Revenue Service. Lawyers can also represent you before the IRS.

✓ Find a financial advisor

Many different types of professionals can assist in developing an investment strategy for any assets you may inherit or setting up a withdrawal plan for surviving beneficiaries from retirement accounts. Which type of professional you should consult depends on what financial advice or help you need.

Financial planners generally take a broad view of your financial affairs. They may develop a comprehensive plan to meet your investment goals or generally advise you on financial matters. They may also manage your investment portfolio. They may charge a set fee for their services or a fee plus commissions on the products you buy.

Investment advisers generally focus on managing your investments. Most are paid by taking a percentage of the assets they manage for you. They may also receive a commission on the investment products they recommend.

Stockbrokers buy and sell stocks and bonds as you direct them to and are paid by commissions on the trades they make for you. Some brokers also provide financial planning services.

Insurance agents can help you with insurance questions and products, including health, long-term care, and life insurance products as well as annuities.

Certified public accountants (CPA) are licensed by a state to offer a variety of accounting services, including tax preparation, financial audits, business valuations, and succession planning for small businesses. CPAs can also represent you before the IRS.

✓ Check on the background of any financial professional

Before hiring any financial professional, always inquire as to what licenses or certifications he or she holds, the types of services offered, the typical clients he or she works with, and how he or she will be compensated. You should always know in advance how much you are going to pay for your financial professional's services. Get in writing whether you are being charged a set fee for each service or transaction or whether you are having a percentage deducted from any transaction. You should also ask if the professional is receiving any additional compensation from any other source for any trades or transactions made for you.

Financial professionals can string a wide range of credentials and certifications after their names. Be sure you know what's behind those credentials. Ask what the professional had to do to gain the credential and if any complaints have been filed against him or her.

Here are places to check on credentials:

- Use www.finra.org/Investors/ToolsCalculators/BrokerCheck/ for information about brokerages, brokers, and investment advisers.
- The Securities and Exchange Commission provides investment advisor information at www.adviserinfo.sec.gov.
- Go to https://eapps.naic.org/cis/ to check on complaints against insurance agents.
- You will find disciplinary actions taken against CPAs by the American Institute of Certified Public Accountants at www.aicpa.org/FORTHEPUBLIC /DISCIPLINARYACTIONS/Pages/default.aspx.

- Check on certified financial planners at http://www.cfp.net/utility/verify-an -individual-s-cfp-certification-and-background.

- Information about any disciplinary history for attorneys can be found at your state bar association's website.

- You can check out the different types of tax preparers at www.irs.gov/Tax -Professionals/Overview-of-Tax-Return-Preparer-Requirements.

Build a Team Action Checklists

Assigned Tasks

❑ I've asked the following people to do these tasks and indicated when they need to be completed.

Task	Who	When
❑ Take care of pets	_____	_____
❑ Develop list of people to contact	_____	_____
❑ Call friends and family	_____	_____
❑ Locate the funeral preneed contract	_____	_____
❑ Select a funeral director	_____	_____
❑ Make funeral arrangements	_____	_____
❑ Locate cemetery deed	_____	_____
❑ Contact the Veterans Administration	_____	_____
❑ Find photos for visual tribute	_____	_____
❑ Identify appropriate charities	_____	_____
❑ Write the obituary	_____	_____
❑ Proof the obituary	_____	_____
❑ Locate the will	_____	_____
❑ Coordinate food for the service	_____	_____
❑ Select speakers and pallbearers	_____	_____

❑   Get copies of death certificate   _____   _____

❑   Arrange for the grave marker   _____   _____

❑   Notify Social Security   _____   _____

❑   Get copies of birth certificate   _____   _____

❑   Get copy of military records (DD-214)   _____   _____

❑   Notify employers   _____   _____

❑   Notify banks   _____   _____

❑   Notify financial advisors   _____   _____

❑   Find a lawyer   _____   _____

❑   Take care of direct deposits   _____   _____

❑   Take care of automatic payments   _____   _____

❑   Locate passwords   _____   _____

❑   Inventory safe deposit box   _____   _____

❑   Locate all pension documents   _____   _____

❑   Locate retirement plans and accounts   _____   _____

❑   Secure/insure the house and car   _____   _____

❑   Contact insurance companies   _____   _____

❑   Notify mortgage company   _____   _____

❑   Notify landlord   _____   _____

❑   Notify tenants   _____   _____

❑   List all credit card accounts   _____   _____

❑   Cancel driver's license   _____   _____

❑   Get copy of credit report   _____   _____

❑   Notify credit bureaus   _____   _____

❑   Freeze social media accounts   _____   _____

❑   Take care of personal possessions   _____   _____

❑   Clean the house or apartment   _____   _____

Financial Professionals

❑   I do not need to contact any financial professionals.

❑   I have contacted the following financial professionals my loved one was using:

Name: _____

Firm: _____

Phone: _____ Fax: _____

Address: _____

_____

E-mail: _____ Website: _____

Account number: _____

Name: _____

Firm: _____

Phone: _____ Fax: _____

Address: _____

_____

E-mail: _____ Website: _____

Account number: _____

Name: _____

Firm: _____

Phone: _____ Fax: _____

Address: _____

_____

E-mail: _____ Website: _____

Account number: _____

❑   I do not need to engage the services of any financial professionals.

❑   I have received recommendations of the following financial professionals:

Name: _____

Firm: _____

Phone: _____ Fax: _____

Address: _____

_____

E-mail: _____ Website: _____

   ❏   I have verified the credentials and complaint history.

Name: _____

Firm: _____

Phone: _____ Fax: _____

Address: _____

_____

E-mail: _____ Website: _____

   ❏   I have verified the credentials and complaint history.

Name: _____

Firm: _____

Phone: _____ Fax: _____

Address: _____

_____

E-mail: _____ Website: _____

   ❏   I have verified the credentials and complaint history.

   ❏   I have identified the following services that I need to receive from the financial professionals.

_____

   ❏   I want to ask the following questions of the financial professionals.

_____

   ❏   I understand how the financial professional will be paid.

_____

   ❏   I have a letter of engagement.

Lawyers

❏   I do not need to contact any lawyers.

❏   I have contacted the following lawyers my loved one was using:

Name: _____

Firm: _____

Phone: _____ Fax: _____

Address: _____

_____

E-mail: _____ Website: _____

Name: _____

Firm: _____

Phone: _____ Fax: _____

Address: _____

_____

E-mail: _____ Website: _____

Name: _____

Firm: _____

Phone: _____ Fax: _____

Address: _____

_____

E-mail: _____ Website: _____

❏   I do not need to engage the services of any lawyers.

❏   I have received recommendations of the following lawyers:

Name: _____

Firm: _____

Phone: _____ Fax: _____

Address: _____

_____

E-mail: _____ Website: _____

❏   I have verified the complaint history with the bar association.

❏   Recommended by: _____

Name: _____

Firm: _____

Phone: _____ Fax: _____

Address: _____

_____

E-mail: _____ Website: _____

❏   I have verified the complaint history with the bar association.

❏   Recommended by: _____

Name: _____

Firm: _____

Phone: _____ Fax: _____

Address: _____

_____

E-mail: _____ Website: _____

❏   I have verified the complaint history with the bar association.

❏   Recommended by: _____

❏   I have identified the following services that I need to receive from the lawyer.

_____

❏   I want to ask the following questions of the lawyer.

_____

❏   I understand how the lawyer will be paid.

_____

_____

❏   I have a letter of engagement.

Build a Team: Other

Other miscellaneous information of interest:

_____

_____

_____

_____

_____

_____

_____

_____

_____

_____

_____

_____

_____

_____

_____

_____

_____

_____

_____

_____

_____

_____

_____

_____

_____

_____

CHAPTER 4
APPLY FOR SURVIVORS' BENEFITS

As a survivor, you may be eligible for benefits from Social Security, the Veterans Administration (VA), workers' compensation, or private and public pension plans. It's important that you investigate all the possible benefits you or others in your family might be able to receive. You may also be entitled to other sources of income or other assistance through various types of insurance, which will be covered in Chapter 7. This chapter is primarily concerned with public benefits that may be available to you as a surviving spouse or child. In June 2013, the United States Supreme Court struck down the provision of the Defense of Marriage Act that defined marriage as between a man and woman for purposes of federal benefits. Now, survivors of same-sex marriages may be entitled to survivors' benefits on the same basis as opposite-sex couples.

My to-do checklist

Done   **Need to Do**

❑　　　❑　　　Notify Social Security of the death

❑　　　❑　　　Apply for Social Security survivors' benefits

❑　　　❑　　　Get copies of birth certificate

❑　　　❑　　　Get copies of marriage license

❑　　　❑　　　Get copies of divorce decree

❑　　　❑　　　Apply for veterans' burial benefits

❑　　　❑　　　Get a copy of military service record (DD 214)

❑　　　❑　　　Request a burial flag

❑　　　❑　　　Request a veteran's burial

❑ ❑ Request a veteran's headstone

❑ ❑ Request military honors

❑ ❑ Get reimbursement for funeral or burial expenses

❑ ❑ Apply for veterans' benefits as a survivor

❑ ❑ Apply for education benefits

❑ ❑ Apply for workers' compensation survivor benefits

❑ ❑ Identify all available pension benefits

❑ ❑ Take disbursements from 401(k) retirement plans

❑ ❑ Take disbursements from individual retirement accounts

❑ ❑ Complete the checklists for Chapter 4

Survivors' benefits action checklists

The Action Checklists in Chapter 4 are set out in the following order:

- *Pensions*
- *Social Security Benefits*
- *Veterans' Benefits*
- *Workers' Compensation*
- *Survivors' Benefits: Other*

✓ Notify Social Security of the death

You can report the death by calling 1-800-772-1213 or TTY 1-800-325-0778 from 7 a.m. to 7 p.m., Monday through Friday. When you call, have the deceased person's Social Security number handy.

You have to return any Social Security checks that are received for the month in which the beneficiary died. For example, if the person dies in July, you must return the July benefit, which is paid in August. If the decedent receives a Social Security check after he or she dies, you have to return the uncashed check. You will also need to notify the bank where the Social Security check is direct-deposited of the death as soon as possible so that the bank can return any Social Security payments.

✓ Apply for Social Security survivors' benefits

Social Security can be an important source of continuing income when your family's earnings are reduced or stopped because of a family member's death. For more information about navigating the Social Security Administration, check out AARP's *Social Security for Dummies* by Jonathan Peterson, at www.aarp.org/SS4Dummies.

Before you can receive monthly cash benefits as a survivor, your family member must have been credited for a certain amount of work under Social Security. For most benefits, the worker must have at least ten years of Social Security-covered employment. For a worker's child or the surviving spouse who cares for that child to be eligible for benefits, however, the worker only needs one and a half years of work in the three years before his or her death.

A number of benefits may be available to you and your family as survivors of a worker who had the sufficient number of years of Social Security-covered benefits.

- As a surviving spouse, you may be entitled to a one-time $255 lump-sum payment.

Social Security survivors insurance can provide cash benefits based on the earnings record of the person who died. You need to have one of the following relationships with the person who died to receive benefits:

- If you are a *surviving spouse*, you can get full benefits at your full retirement age or reduced benefits as early as age 60.
- If you are a *disabled spouse*, you are eligible for benefits as early as age 50.
- If you are a *surviving spouse* and you take care of the deceased worker's child who is under age 16 or disabled before age 22 and who is receiving Social Security benefits, you can receive benefits at any age.
- If you *remarry* before the age of 60 (age 50 if you are disabled), you lose your survivor benefit.
- If you are *divorced* from the worker, you get the same benefits as if you were still married as long as you were married for at least ten years. The benefit paid to you will not affect the benefits received by other survivors unless you are taking care of the worker's surviving child.
- If you are the unmarried *child* of a worker who died and are under age 18 or are up to age 19 and are attending high school full time, you will get benefits. Under certain circumstances, benefits can be paid to stepchildren, grandchildren, or adopted children.
- If your parent died and you were *disabled* before age 22 and remain disabled, you will get benefits at any age.
- If you are the *parent* of a deceased worker and depended on the worker for at least half of your support, you will get benefits.

The amount you receive depends on the worker's earnings, how long he or she paid into Social Security, your age, and the type of survivor benefit you receive.

The importance of full retirement age: Full retirement age for Social Security retirement is the age at which people receive the standard benefit. It used to be age 65, but it is now gradually increasing to age 67 for people born in 1938 and later. People can still start receiving Social Security at age 62, but at a significantly reduced amount.

- If the deceased worker was receiving Social Security at the reduced rate, the survivors' benefits will also be reduced.

- If the surviving spouse starts receiving survivor benefits before his or her full retirement age, that benefit will also be reduced. As a surviving spouse, you may have a different full retirement age if you want to take benefits on your own record.

The rules are confusing and depend on your individual circumstances. Check with a Social Security representative at www.socialsecurity.gov/reach.htm.

How to Apply for Social Security Survivor Benefits

If you are already receiving Social Security benefits on your spouse's or your parent's record, you need to report the death to Social Security. Call 1-800-772-1213 (TTY 1-800-325-0778) or visit your local Social Security office.

If you are already receiving retirement or disability benefits on your own work record, you should speak to a Social Security representative to make sure that you receive the benefit that pays you the most.

If you or your children are not receiving any Social Security benefits, you need to make an appointment to talk with a Social Security representative at your local office. You can find those addresses at the SSA web site www.ssa.gov or in the blue pages of your telephone book.

You will need to bring the following documents with you:

- Proof of death (either from funeral home or death certificate)
- Your Social Security number and the deceased family member's number
- Your birth certificate (original or certified copy)
- Your marriage certificate if you are the widow or widower (original or certified copy)
- Proof of U.S. citizenship or lawful alien status if you were born outside the United States
- Your divorce papers if you are applying as a surviving divorced spouse (certified copy)

- Dependent children's Social Security numbers and birth certificates, if available
- Deceased worker's most recent W-2 forms or federal self-employment tax return
- The name of your bank and your account and routing numbers so that your benefits can be directly deposited into your account

Do not delay making the appointment because the sooner you apply, the sooner the benefits will start. Social Security will help you locate documents if you can't find them all.

You can find details on specific requirements at www.ssa.gov or at any Social Security Administration office located throughout the country.

Note: Because the Social Security Act is amended from time to time, this information may not be the latest concerning benefits that you, as a survivor, may be entitled to. Contact the nearest Social Security Administration office for a full explanation of your rights under the law.

Make copies and more copies: It's a good idea to make several copies of all these documents. You will need to present many of the same documents to government agencies, financial institutions, and who knows where else. You *never* want to leave behind or mail an original document. Chances are good that some document is going to get misplaced and you'll need to present it again.

✓ Get copies of birth certificate

✓ Get copies of marriage license

Tracking down originals or certified copies of birth, marriage, or divorce records can be a time-consuming task.

Each state has its own method of maintaining records of births and marriages. They can usually be obtained from the county clerk, registrar, or recorder of the county in which the birth or marriage took place.

Many states have a central clearinghouse generally called the Department of Vital Statistics. The Centers for Disease Control and Prevention has a useful website with information on how and where to write to obtain these records in each state at www.cdc.gov/nchs/w2w.htm.

To expedite the sometimes lengthy procedure of obtaining the certificates, it is a good idea to first find out how much each certificate or certified copy will cost. Fees generally range from $2 to $20. Additional copies may be available at reduced rates. Once you know the cost, you can write for the copies you need, enclosing the necessary payment.

To be a "certified copy," it must have a statement by an official that it is a true copy of an original.

Many states will not issue copies of birth or marriage certificates unless the requestor is closely related to the person named in the certificate. Therefore, when requesting records for someone else in your family, it is important to identify yourself as spouse, parent, or child.

✓ Get copies of divorce decree

You obtain certified copies of a divorce decree, qualified domestic relations order (QDRO), or annulment order from the clerk or registrar of the court that granted the divorce or annulment. Once again, the fee for obtaining copies varies in each state and may also depend on the number of pages in the document.

Write a letter to the court that granted the decree, order, or judgment to inquire about the cost of obtaining a copy of the document. Note the date and year that the divorce or annulment was granted and be sure to enclose a self-addressed, stamped envelope.

✓ Apply for veteran's burial benefits

The Department of Veterans Affairs is charged with administering benefits available to persons who have served on active duty in the U.S. military service. Many services and benefits are available to the family of an eligible veteran.

The available benefits depend on the veteran's length of service, the era during which the service was performed, whether the veteran is disabled, whether the disability was caused by active service, and many other criteria. Certain of these benefits are available to survivors if the veteran was separated from the service under conditions other than dishonorable.

You will need to have documentation of your family member's military service to apply for any benefits available to the veteran and to you as a surviving family member. Here's the documentation you should have:

- Full name and military rank
- Branch of service
- Social Security number
- Service number
- VA claim number, if applicable
- Date and place of birth
- Date and place of death
- Date of retirement or last separation from active duty
- Copy of any military separation documents, such as the Department of Defense Form 214 (DD 214)

✓ Get a copy of military service record (DD 214)

The DD 214 will specify that the veteran was on active military duty and will show that release from active duty was under other than dishonorable conditions. You can get this very important record at www.archives.gov/veterans/military-service-records/.

✓ Request a burial flag

An American flag may be issued to drape over the casket of an eligible veteran. After the funeral service, the flag will be given to the next of kin or close friend or associate. Flags are issued at any VA office and most local post offices. A Presidential Memorial Certificate is also available at no cost to the family.

✓ Request a veteran's burial

Burial in a national cemetery is open to all members of the armed forces and veterans having met minimum active service duty requirements and having been discharged under conditions other than dishonorable. You as a spouse, a widow or widower, minor children, and, under certain conditions, unmarried adult children are also eligible for burial in a national cemetery. In most cases, one gravesite is provided for the burial of all eligible family members, and a single headstone or marker is provided. When both you and your spouse are veterans, you can request two gravesites and two headstones or markers. Certain members of the armed forces reserve components may also be eligible for burial. In each instance, space must be available. There is no charge for the grave plot, its opening and closing, a grave liner, or perpetual care.

✓ Request a veteran's headstone

The VA will furnish a government headstone or marker to be placed at the grave of a veteran at any cemetery around the world. Even if the grave was previously marked, you can obtain a government headstone. This service is provided for eligible veterans, whether they are buried in a national cemetery or elsewhere. A headstone or marker is automatically furnished if burial is in a national cemetery. Otherwise, you must apply to the VA. The VA will ship the headstone or marker, without charge, to the person or firm designated on the application. The VA will also furnish a medallion, on request, to place on an existing headstone or marker that indicates that the person was a veteran. You must pay the cost of setting the headstone or marker or attaching the medallion.

✓ Request military honors

By law, every eligible veteran may receive a military funeral honors ceremony, to include folding and presenting the United States burial flag and the playing of "Taps." A military funeral honors detail consists of two or more uniformed military persons, with at least one being a member of the veteran's branch of the armed forces. The Department of Defense program, "Honoring Those Who Served," calls for funeral directors to request military funeral honors on behalf of the family. Veterans' organizations may assist in providing military funeral honors. In support of this program, VA national cemetery staff can help coordinate military funeral honors at either a national or a private cemetery. For more information, go to http://www.cem.va.gov /military_funeral_honors.asp.

✓ Get reimbursed for funeral or burial expenses

The VA is authorized to pay an allowance toward an eligible veteran's funeral and burial expenses. If it was a service-related death, the VA will pay up to $2,000 toward burial expenses. If the veteran is to be buried in a VA national cemetery, some of or all the cost of transporting the body to the cemetery may be reimbursed. For a nonservice-related death, the VA will pay up to $300 toward burial and funeral expenses and a $300 plot-interment allowance. If the death happens while the veteran was in a VA hospital or under VA contracted nursing home care, some of or all the costs for transporting the remains may be reimbursed.

✓ Apply for veterans' benefits as a survivor

A spouse, unmarried children, and low-income parents may be eligible for Dependency and Indemnity Compensation (DIC) if the family member died during active duty or if the death was service connected. The amount of the basic benefit is determined by the service member's military pay grade. Payments are also made for children under age 18 or up to age 23 who are attending school.

A surviving spouse and unmarried children under age 18 or up to age 23 who are attending school may be eligible for a pension if their income does not exceed certain limits.

✓ Apply for education benefits

If your family member dies as a result of military service, the VA will generally (but with some exceptions) pay to help educate the widow or widower and each son and daughter beyond the secondary school level, including college, graduate school, technical and vocational schools, apprenticeships, and on-the-job training programs. Education loans are also available.

Help applying for VA benefits: You can get assistance in applying for available benefits through the Department of Veterans Affairs. For comprehensive information about veterans' benefits, request a copy of the *Federal Benefits Manual for Veterans and Dependents* from your local VA office. Survivors can also contact the Office of Survivors at www.va.gov/SURVIVORS/index.asp.

✓ Apply for workers' compensation death benefits

All states have adopted workers' compensation laws. Although their details vary greatly, the general purpose of workers' compensation programs is to provide income to and pay the medical expenses for workers who are unable to work as a result of an injury or occupational disease while employed. Additionally, if the worker dies as a result of work-related injury or occupational disease, you as a surviving spouse are entitled to payments for a specified number of years or until your remarriage, whichever is sooner. Your dependent children are entitled to benefits until they reach a certain age. Ordinarily, the laws also provide that the spouse is entitled to a specific funeral or death benefit. Contact your state workers' compensation board to find out if you are eligible and how to apply.

✓ Identify all available pension benefits

Many public and private employees are provided pensions through their jobs. Some pensions are entirely financed by the employer; others are cofinanced by the employer and the employee. Pensions are a way to accumulate tax-advantaged savings that can be used for a steady stream of income when someone is no longer working. Pensions are considered to be defined benefit plans because employees who participate in the pension receive a specific amount of money when they retire. A person's pension amount is based on a formula that includes his or her salary history and how many years he or she was vested in the pension. "Vesting" happens after a set number of years of employment, such as five years on the job. At the time that the individual begins to receive a pension, he or she can elect if the surviving spouse is to continue to receive a portion of the pension after the pensioner's death. Spouses must consent to someone else being named as a beneficiary.

Although many employers are no longer offering pensions, it's important for you as a surviving spouse or beneficiary to locate any possible pensions. You should check with all past employers that offered pension plans during your loved one's employment to determine if you could receive any payments as a survivor or beneficiary. Also search the website of the U.S. Pension Benefit Guaranty Corporation for any earned but unclaimed pensions at http://search.pbgc.gov.

✓ Take disbursements from 401(k) retirement plans

In place of offering a pension, many employers offer 401(k) retirement plans that defer taxes on the contributions both the employee and the employer make and on the plan's earnings until the employee withdraws funds from the plan, usually on retirement. Refer to Chapter 6 on investments for more details about these plans.

These 401(k) plans are called defined contribution plans. The employee makes a specific dollar contribution with each paycheck to a personal plan account. The plan invests those contributions (and the employer's, if any) in mutual funds or other investments that the employee selects from the plan's menu of investment choices. The plan account is credited with any returns on the investment. Unlike fixed pension payments, the amount the employee receives depends on the performance (which may be positive or negative) of the investments. At the time the employee begins to withdraw money from the 401(k), he or she may have the option to take a reduced payment so that the surviving spouse can continue to receive a portion of the retirement funds after the employee's death.

You will want to notify the 401(k) plan administrator of your loved one's death and to apply for any benefits. You will—again—need copies of the death certificate and proof of your relationship, such as your marriage license.

✓ Take disbursements from individual retirement accounts

You should also check for any IRAs that your loved one contributed to. As of 2013, the law allows a person who is under age 70½ and who has earned income to deposit up to $5,500 into an IRA account each year ($6,500 for people over age 50). Contributions to a traditional IRA may be wholly or partially tax deductible or nondeductible, depending on whether the employee is also covered by a qualified pension plan or a 401(k), tax filing status, and income level. IRAs defer taxes on earnings from contributions until funds are withdrawn. Tax penalties apply to early withdrawals except in certain circumstances. Roth IRA contributions are not deductible, but withdrawals are tax-free.

Several other tax-deferred plans can also help put off taxes until retirement. Those who were self-employed may have established a Keogh plan, which allowed for larger, tax-deferred yearly contributions and greater benefits than does an IRA. A SIMPLE IRA is a simplified plan, similar to a 401(k) plan, but with lower contribution limits and less costly administration than a Keogh. Another tax-deferred retirement for self-employed people is a simplified employee pension plan, or SEP, which is a type of IRA. Refer to Chapter 6 on investments for more details about these accounts.

As a surviving spouse or named beneficiary to one or more of these plans, you may be eligible for a substantial payoff or a stream of income. According to the Employee Retirement Income Security Act, surviving spouses must receive some benefits.

- If your spouse was not yet retired when he or she died, you will receive an annuity unless you and your spouse had both signed a waiver. Depending on your spouse's plan, you may have to wait to receive the benefit until the time when your spouse would have first been able to retire.

- If your spouse was already retired, he or she had to make a choice at the time of retirement to not allow you to receive an annuity, and you had to agree by signing a waiver to this benefit. Married people who retire usually elect to take payments as *joint and survivor* beneficiaries. By doing so, the married couple jointly receives a slightly smaller monthly amount, but when either spouse dies, the survivor continues to receive half of that amount until that spouse dies. This setup ensures that the surviving spouse continues to receive a stream of income for life.

- People who are married must have their spouse's written and notarized consent to eliminate the surviving spouse benefit or to name someone other than a spouse as the beneficiary.

- If you are divorced from the plan participant, the plan must recognize how you and your former spouse decided to split the retirement plan benefits. You will need to file the qualified domestic relations order (QDRO) with the plan administrator.

- If your spouse died before age 70½, you will be subject to special tax rules as the beneficiary of a 401(k) or IRA. In brief, the entire amount in the account must be distributed to you either within five years of your spouse's death or over your lifetime starting no later than one year following your spouse's death. You will need to use the specific IRS life expectancy tables to calculate withdrawals and taxes. Be sure to seek expert and timely advice on how best to manage this inheritance.

Federal employees can contribute to a Thrift Savings Plan (TSP) as their defined contribution retirement account. You'll need to notify the plan of the participant's death.

- If the participant was an active federal employee or a member of the uniformed services, report the death to the participant's employing agency or service.

- Otherwise, report the participant's death to the TSP by calling 1-877-968-3778. Press 3 from the main menu and hold to speak to a TSP service representative.

Go to https://www.tsp.gov/lifeevents/death/notifying.shtml to obtain Form TSP 17 (Information Relating to Deceased Participant).

1. Attach the participant's certified death certificate
2. Mail the completed form and the required documentation to:

TSP Death Benefits Processing Unit
P.O. Box 4450
Fairfax, VA 22038-4450

For overnight delivery, mail the form to:

ATTN: TSP Death Benefits Processing Unit
12210 Fairfax Town Center
Unit 906
Fairfax, VA 22033

The importance of being a beneficiary: Anyone creating a retirement plan has the option to name a beneficiary. The beneficiary is the individual who is to receive any remaining balance in the plan at the death of the person who established and contributed to the plan.

- More than one person can be named as a beneficiary. There can be a *primary beneficiary*, who is first in line to receive any benefit; *cobeneficiaries* who share according to the percentages set by the creator of the plan; or *secondary beneficiary* or beneficiaries who receive any benefit only if the primary beneficiary is not alive at the time of the creator's death.

- Beneficiaries have no control of or access to any of the plan's benefits while the creator is alive. Their legal interest is only in the expectation that they will receive something after the creator's death. What they receive depends on the terms of the document, such as the percentage they are eligible to receive if there are other beneficiaries of the same class. Secondary beneficiaries are in the same class and can receive a benefit only if there are no surviving primary beneficiaries.

- The beneficiary has to live longer than the creator or other beneficiaries in their same class. If a beneficiary dies, his or her interest in the benefit goes away. For example, John names Mary as his primary beneficiary and names Jill and Jim as secondary beneficiaries, with Jill getting 75 percent and Jim getting 25 percent. If Mary is alive when John dies, Mary gets 100 percent, and Jill and Jim get nothing. If Mary and Jill both die before John, Jim gets 100 percent.

- Naming someone as a beneficiary of a retirement plan is different from naming someone as a beneficiary in a will. The terms of the retirement plan document take priority over the terms of the will. For example, Mary names John as the primary beneficiary of her 401(k) plan and names Susan as the primary beneficiary in her will. On Mary's death, John receives all the assets in the retirement plan; Susan receives no part of the 401(k).

- If creator is married, the spouse must consent to the naming of a beneficiary other than the spouse.

Survivors' Benefits Quick Tips

Apply for Social Security survivors' benefits

You will need:

- Proof of death (either from funeral home or death certificate)
- Your Social Security number and the deceased family member's number
- Your birth certificate (original or certified copy)
- Your marriage certificate if you are the widow or widower (original or certified copy)
- Proof of U.S. citizenship or lawful alien status if you were born outside the United States
- Your divorce papers if you are applying as a surviving divorced spouse (certified copy)
- Dependent children's Social Security numbers and birth certificates, if available
- Deceased worker's most recent W-2 forms or federal self-employment tax return
- The name of your bank and your account number so that your benefits can be directly deposited into your account

Apply for Social Security benefits for any dependent children

You will need:

- The deceased worker's Social Security card or a record of the number
- Your children's birth certificates and Social Security numbers
- Adoption papers if the child was adopted

Apply for veterans' burial benefits

- You should have the funeral home contact the national cemetery where you want interment or if you want a headstone, grave marker, or service medallion.
- If possible, the following information concerning the deceased should be provided when the cemetery is first contacted:
  - Full name and military rank
  - Branch of service
  - Social Security number
  - Service number
  - VA claim number, if applicable
  - Date and place of birth
  - Date and place of death

- Date of retirement or last separation from active duty

- Copy of any military separation document, such as the Department of Defense Form 214 (DD 214). The discharge documents must specify active military duty and show that release from active duty was under other than dishonorable conditions.

- **Get a copy of the veteran's service record**. You can order this record, called the DD 214, at www.archives.gov/veterans/military-service-records/.

- **Order a flag** at www.va.gov/vaforms/ (VA Form 21-2008) or contact your local VA office or U.S. Post Office. Most funeral directors will be able to help you obtain a flag.

- **Apply for burial benefits** by filling out VA Form 21-530, *Application for Burial Benefits*. You should attach a copy of the veteran's military discharge document (DD 214 or equivalent), death certificate, and funeral and burial bills. These bills should show that you have paid them in full. You may download the form at www.va.gov/vaforms/.

- **Contact your local VA office** for help in obtaining burial benefits or go to www.cem.va.gov/.

- **Apply for survivors' benefits** by providing the following to your local VA office:

  - The veteran's DD 214 number

  - A copy of the service record

Apply for workers' compensation survivors' benefits

- If the decedent was receiving workers' compensation at the time of death, ask the state workers' compensation board to determine if a widow, widower, or dependent children can continue to receive benefits.

- If the decedent's death was caused by an injury or illness while working, ask the state workers' compensation board to determine if a widow, widower, or dependent children are eligible for any compensation.

Apply for pension benefits for survivors

- Contact each former employer who offered a pension to the decedent to claim any survivors' benefits.

- Check for unclaimed pensions at U.S. Pension Benefit Guaranty Corporation's online directory at http://search.pbgc.gov.

Take disbursements from retirement plans

- Contact the plan manager for any 401(k) or individual retirement accounts (IRAs) to determine the steps that surviving beneficiaries need to take.

Survivors' Benefits Action Checklists

Pensions

- ❑ There are no pension plans.
- ❑ I have contacted the following pension plans.
- ❑ I have delivered the death certificate.

Pension source: _____

Name of payor: _____

Phone: _____ Fax: _____

Address: _____

_____

E-mail: _____ Website: _____

Pension ID #: _____

- ❑ There are benefits to survivors under this plan.
- ❑ There are no benefits to survivors under this plan.

Pension source: _____

Name of payor: _____

Phone: _____ Fax: _____

Address: _____

_____

E-mail: _____ Website: _____

Pension ID #: _____

❑   There are benefits to survivors under this plan.

❑   There are no benefits to survivors under this plan.

Social Security Benefits

❑ I notified the Social Security Administration (1-800-772-1213) of the death on

_____.

❑ I have an appointment with a Social Security representative to discuss benefits on

_____.

❑ I have applied for Social Security survivor benefits.

❑ There are no available Social Security survivor benefits.

❑ The deceased worked in the railroad industry at any time after January 1, 1937.*

❑ The deceased did not work in the railroad industry at any time after January 1, 1937.

Name on Social Security card: _____

Social Security number: _____

Type of monthly Social Security benefit the deceased worker was receiving: _____

_____

(*Disability, Retirement, Widow, etc.*)

Monthly Social Security benefit amount the deceased worker was receiving: _____

❑ I am eligible for the $255 Social Security survivor benefit.

❑ I have received the $255 Social Security survivor benefit.

❑ I have applied for Social Security widow/widower benefits.

❑ I have applied for Social Security benefits as a disabled spouse.

❑ I have applied for Social Security benefits as a divorced spouse.

❑ I have applied for Social Security benefits for dependent children.

❑ I have applied for Social Security benefits for dependent parents.

This answer may affect the amount of Social Security you receive.

Veterans' Benefits

- ❑ The deceased did not serve in the military service of the United States.
- ❑ I or other family members may be eligible for veterans' benefits.
- ❑ I have a copy of the DD 214.
- ❑ I have requested a burial flag.
- ❑ I have requested burial in a national cemetery.
- ❑ I have requested a veteran's headstone.
- ❑ I have requested military honors at the burial.
- ❑ I have asked for reimbursement of funeral or burial expenses.
- ❑ I have applied for VA benefits for myself as a surviving spouse.
- ❑ I have applied for VA benefits for our children.
- ❑ I have applied for educational benefits.

Name deceased served under:

_____

| *First* | *Middle* | *Last* |

Entered Active Service			Separated		
Date	**Place**	**Service Number**	**Date**	**Place**	**Grade or Rank and Branch**

Workers' Compensation

- ❏ The deceased was not receiving workers' compensation benefits.
- ❏ The deceased's death may have been caused by an injury or illness on the job.
- ❏ I may be eligible for workers' compensation benefits as a survivor.
- ❏ I have contacted the workers' compensation bureau.

Employer: _____

Phone: _____ Fax: _____

Address: _____

_____

E-mail: _____ Website: _____

****

Date of injury or occupational disease: _____

Insurance company: _____

Phone: _____ Fax: _____

Address: _____

_____

E-mail: _____ Website: _____

Claim #: _____

Details of injury or occupational disease: _____

****

State bureau for workers' compensation: _____

Phone: _____ Fax: _____

Contact Person: _____

Address: _____

_____

E-mail: _____ Website: _____

Survivors' Benefits: Other

Other miscellaneous information of interest:

_____

_____

_____

_____

_____

_____

_____

_____

_____

_____

_____

_____

_____

_____

_____

_____

_____

_____

_____

_____

_____

_____

_____

_____

_____

_____

_____

_____

_____

CHAPTER 5
FIND OUT WHAT'S AT THE BANK

Banks used to be quite straightforward. They offered checking and savings accounts, lent money to buy homes and cars, and maybe gave you a toaster when you opened a new account. Today, banks and credit unions provide a proliferation of services and offer multiple types of accounts. In addition to a checking account and a savings account, your loved one might have had a certificate of deposit (CD) or money market account, carried a credit card or debit card with a PIN (personal identification number), used a financial advisor housed in the bank, relied on the automatic teller machine (ATM) to transfer funds between accounts and get cash, and paid bills online. Instead of the bank being down the street where you're greeted by a teller you've known for years, it now could be totally online and many states away. You will need to track down all the different types of accounts and information on where they are located, account numbers, PINs, balances, and so forth.

Once you've identified the accounts, you need to review how the account is titled. Is it a joint account with right of survivorship, a pay on death (POD) account, convenience account, or only in the name of your loved one? How the account is titled makes a big difference in what happens to the account after the death of an owner and who is entitled to the balance.

My to-do checklist

Done	Need to Do	
❏	❏	Notify all banks and credit unions of the death and provide a copy of the death certificate
❏	❏	Assemble account numbers and determine PINs, ATM passwords, and online banking usernames and passwords
❏	❏	Review how bank accounts are titled
❏	❏	Document your authority
❏	❏	Determine what to do about direct deposits and payments

❑ ❑ Redeem all savings bonds

❑ ❑ Access and inventory any safe-deposit boxes

❑ ❑ Complete the checklists for Chapter 5

Banking action checklists

The Action Checklists in Chapter 5 are set out in the following order:

- *Certificates of Deposit*
- *Checking Accounts*
- *Credit Union Accounts*
- *Safe-Deposit Boxes*
- *Savings Accounts*
- *Savings Bonds*
- *Banking: Other*

✓ **Notify all banks and credit unions of the death and provide a copy of the death certificate**

Bank Accounts Commercial banks offer a wide range of services. They handle savings and checking accounts and make short- and long-term loans for personal and business use. Many also provide estate and investment services.

Checking accounts are considered **demand deposits**. They allow you to draw checks payable to anyone. Many financial institutions now offer interest-bearing checking accounts along with traditional fee-based checking plans. Banks may also offer overdraft protection by linking your checking account to your savings account. Most banks charge stiff fees for each overdrawn check, however. Some may also charge a fee for overdraft protection. During these uncertain and unsettling times following a death in the family, you'll need to make sure accounts aren't overdrawn.

Savings accounts are another type of **demand deposit**. In other words, the depositor has the right to demand or to withdraw any of or all the funds at any time during regular banking hours. Savings accounts pay interest, which is noted, along with deposits and withdrawals, on a periodic statement or available online. A **money market savings account** pays a higher rate of interest than a standard savings account but may require a certain minimum balance in the account.

Certificates of deposit are **time deposits**. Customers who use CDs agree to leave their money in the bank for a certain period (for example, two years). During that time, the customer may not withdraw those funds without incurring significant interest penalties. In return for having this long-term use of the money, banks generally pay a higher rate of interest. You will need to talk to the manager to determine if the early withdrawal penalty can be waived if you need to cash out a CD early to pay for death expenses.

Credit Union Accounts Although they are organized differently from banking institutions, credit unions work very much like banks. Typically, you need to be a member of some identified group to have an account, but in turn you become a part owner of the credit union. Credit unions offer services that encourage members to save and often provide their members loans at lower rates than banks do. They offer checking and savings accounts (although they may be called share or draft accounts), credit cards, and online banking. Federally chartered credit unions are regulated by the National Credit Union Administration.

✓ **Assemble account numbers and determine PINs, ATM passwords, and online banking usernames and passwords**

With today's multiple ways to do banking, we can accumulate a sometimes bewildering collection of cards, PINs, passwords, and usernames. They are the keys to banking without ever entering a bank. We use them to get cash from an ATM or transfer funds and pay bills via online banking.

If your loved one has not left clear and detailed information about all the banks and banking services he or she used and you don't know where to find a secure list of PINs, passwords, and usernames, your task in assembling this information has the potential of being one of your most difficult, frustrating, and time-consuming chores.

For the very good reason of protecting the security of their customers' accounts, banks are going to insist that you have all the appropriate documentation to justify releasing any account information about or funds from the accounts of a deceased customer. Upon learning of the death of an account holder, a bank may automatically freeze any activity within an account. A bank is properly concerned about the potential of some unauthorized person raiding the funds before it can determine who should have access to the account. It may seem frustrating to face a lot of bureaucratic details during a trying time, but it is for the protection of the account holder, the rightful owners, and the bank. Don't do anything as foolish (and criminal) as forging the deceased's signature to a check to get some quick cash.

You may need to do some detective work to track down all bank and credit union accounts. Look around the home and desk for checkbooks and bank statements for bank names, branch address, and account numbers. Watch the mail for bank statements. Check the most recent tax returns for any reported interest from interest-bearing accounts. There are lots of stories about people who had multiple accounts scattered in different banks in other towns because they didn't want any one bank to know how much money they had. If your loved one did any online banking, you should find e-mails with bank statements or alerts. Of course, before you can search for online account information, you'll need the computer password, and then you will need the account password and PIN. Refer to the section on digital assets in Chapter 10 for tips on how to find these items.

✓ **Review how bank accounts are titled**

It is important for you to know about all the various ways bank accounts can be owned, or "titled," so that you can understand who is entitled to any funds in the account. How the account is titled makes a big difference as to who gets the money.

Joint Ownership Among the possible ways a bank account can be titled are the following:

- Individual account: Money remaining in this account will be distributed according to the terms of the will. If there is no will, it will become part of the overall estate and be distributed to surviving heirs.

- Agency or convenience account: Money in this type of account can be accessed by the cosigner on the account but it does not belong to the cosigner on the death of the owner. In other words, a cosigner is not a co-owner. This type of account is what most people use if they want a family member to have access to the account to help pay bills when they are out of town or in the hospital. Money remaining in this account will be distributed according to the terms of the will, or to surviving heirs.

- Joint with right of survivorship account: As soon as this type of account is created, all money in the account belongs to both joint owners. On the death of one of the owners, the account automatically goes to the surviving co-owner. Adding a spouse, child, or any other person to the account as joint owner is the same as making a gift of all money then on deposit and any future deposits. The joint owner can write checks for any purpose and can withdraw it to zero. When a joint owner dies, however, the bank may want to put a temporary freeze on the account until everything is documented.

- Pay on death (POD) account: The person named as beneficiary on this type of account is automatically entitled to receive the balance in the account on the owner's death. The named beneficiary has no right to the money or authority to access the account until then.

✓ **Document your authority**

Once you have identified a bank account, you should call or make an appointment to speak with a manager to let the bank know of the death. Ask what documentation the bank will need to close or make disbursements from the account. Most likely, you will need a certified copy of the death certificate for every bank. You will also need proper documentation of your authority to act on the account, such as your letters of administration that you receive from the probate court. If there is a will, you'll first need to go to the court to receive what are typically called Letters Testamentary, which will authorize the executor to act on behalf of the decedent. If there's no will, the court will appoint what's called the personal representative, or administrator. Refer to Chapter 11 for more information about probate and letters of administration. Depending on the state, bank, and type of account, the bank may wait for orders from the court before releasing some of or all the funds.

Remember that if you were acting on behalf of the deceased person as an agent with powers of attorney, your authority vanished on the death of the deceased. All powers of attorney, even if they are durable, become void documents on the death of the person who granted the powers. Things that you could do as agent you can no longer do.

If the deceased had Social Security benefits directly deposited to the account, the Social Security Administration will code the account with a Death Notification Entry, which will stop the monthly payments to the account and may serve as documentation of the death.

The last Social Security check: The Social Security benefit received for the month in which the beneficiary died cannot be kept. For example, the beneficiary dies on July 31. Because he or she did not live for the entire month of July, the check issued in August for the month of July will have to be refunded. The bank will need to refund any direct deposit or the United States Treasury will reverse the deposit. Checks that turn up in the mail after the beneficiary's death must be returned to the U.S. government.

If you are a named beneficiary or a joint owner on the account, you will also need to prove your identity. You will need to either establish a new account with a new account number, direct the bank where to deposit the funds electronically, or request a check for the balance. As a surviving joint owner, you should continue to have access to the funds, but you will still need to provide the required documentation. You should consider removing the deceased's name from any account on which you are a joint owner and signing a new signature card.

✓ Determine what to do about direct deposits and payments

While you are at the bank, you'll need to pay attention to any direct deposits paid into the account that need to be or will automatically be stopped such as pay checks from employers and Social Security benefits as well as any automatic payments such as for the mortgage, car loans, utilities, cable, and telephone. The bank will stop those automatic payments, so you will need to notify those companies of the death and make new arrangements for payments, if they need to continue.

✓ Redeem all savings bonds

Determine if your loved one had a list of each government savings bond he or she held. You'll want to know the type series (E, EE, H, HH, or I), denomination, issue date, and names on the bond. You can use the Treasury Hunt tool at www.savingsbonds.gov/indiv /tools/tools_treasuryhunt.htm to find out how much each bond is worth today.

You also need to know if the savings bonds are paper or electronic. If the person who died had an online TreasuryDirect account, you need to contact the Bureau of Public Debt at www.treasurydirect.gov/email.htm.

Bonds, like bank accounts, can be owned either individually or jointly. If there is no survivor named on the bond and if no court is involved, to claim any paper bond you will need to fill out Form PD F 5336, sign the form in the presence of a certifying officer, and mail the form, the bonds, and a copy of the death certificate to the Bureau of the Public Debt, PO Box 7012, Parkersburg, WV 26106-7012. If a court is involved in settling the estate (and one must be involved in any event if the bonds total more than $100,000), including if the estate is being handled through "small estate administration," it gets a bit more complicated. The Treasury Department website at www.treasurydirect.gov/indiv/research/indepth/ebonds/res_e_bonds_eedeath.htm can walk you through the detailed steps. The interest will need to be reported on the federal income tax return filed for the year in which the owner died and the bonds were cashed in unless the taxpayer reported the interest as it was earned on previous returns.

✓ Access and inventory any safe-deposit boxes

Safe-deposit boxes provide a place for storing valuables and documents at a small cost. Most banks rent safe-deposit boxes or provide them as a free service along with a checking or savings account. You'll need to identify the location of all safe-deposit boxes because they may contain stocks, bonds, gold, silver, coins, jewelry, cash, and other valuables that you'll want to know about. They may also contain important papers such as wills, marriage licenses, birth certificates, deeds to real estate, burial plot deeds, car titles, and insurance policies that you need to locate.

State laws and banking procedures are designed to protect the property in the box from unauthorized access. Thus, you will need to check with the bank where the box is located for the procedures you need to follow to get access to the box. For example, according to Georgia law, if you have a copy of a death certificate, you can open and examine what's in a safe-deposit box in the presence of a bank official to determine if it contains a will, burial deed, or insurance policy. Nothing else can be removed. The next step is to get a court order permitting an inventory of the contents of the box in the presence of a bank official. There will need to be another order from the court allowing the person named in the order to remove any contents of the box.

A safe-deposit box, like a bank account, can be owned individually or jointly. If you are a joint owner, you will have access to the box, but you'll need to follow the required procedures to conduct the inventory and report the contents to the court. This process ensures that the court can oversee the proper distribution of the box's contents and that any applicable taxes are applied to the items. Although joint owners of a safe-deposit box have access to the box, access does not mean that you own the contents of the box. Finding a diamond ring in a jointly owned safe-deposit box does not make the ring a gift to you. It will be part of the ring owner's probate estate. If you have any questions about the rights of a safe-deposit box co-owner, check with your bank or your attorney.

Banking Action Checklists

Certificates of Deposit

❏ There are no certificates of deposit (CDs).

❏ I have identified the following certificates of deposit (CDs):

Name of institution: _____

Phone: _____ Fax: _____

Address: _____

_____

E-mail: _____ Website: _____

Account #: _____

Maturity date: _____

Principal amount: _____

Owners: _____

Name of institution: _____

Phone: _____ Fax: _____

Address: _____

_____

E-mail: _____ Website: _____

Account #: _____

Maturity date: _____

Principal amount: _____

Owners: _____

Checking Accounts

❑ There are no checking accounts.

❑ I have identified the following checking accounts and notified the institution of the death:

Name of institution: _____

Phone: _____ Fax: _____

Address: _____

_____

E-mail: _____ Website: _____

Account number: _____

Owner(s): _____

Name of institution: _____

Phone: _____ Fax: _____

Address: _____

_____

E-mail: _____ Website: _____

Account number: _____

Owner(s): _____

Name of institution: _____

Phone: _____ Fax: _____

Address: _____

_____

E-mail: _____ Website: _____

Account number: _____

Owner(s): _____

Name of institution: _____

Phone: _____ Fax: _____

Address: _____

_____

E-mail: _____ Website: _____

Account number: _____

Owner(s): _____

Name of institution: _____

Phone: _____ Fax: _____

Address: _____

_____

E-mail: _____ Website: _____

Account number: _____

Owner(s): _____

Credit Union Accounts

❏   There are no credit union accounts.

❏   I have identified the following credit union accounts and notified the institution of the death:

Name of institution: _____

Phone: _____ Fax: _____

Address: _____

_____

E-mail: _____ Website: _____

Account number: _____

Name of institution: _____

Phone: _____ Fax: _____

Address: _____

_____

E-mail: _____ Website: _____

Account number: _____

Name of institution: _____

Phone: _____ Fax: _____

Address: _____

_____

E-mail: _____ Website: _____

Account number: _____

Safe-Deposit Boxes

❑   There are no safe-deposit boxes.

❑   I have identified the following safe-deposit boxes and notified the institution of the death:

Name of institution: _____

Phone: _____ Fax: _____

Address: _____

_____

E-mail: _____ Website: _____

Box number: _____

Key location: _____

Notes on steps to inventory and access contents: _____

_____

Name of institution: _____

Phone: _____ Fax: _____

Address: _____

_____

E-mail: _____ Website: _____

Box number: _____

Key location: _____

Notes on steps to inventory and access contents: _____

_____

Name of institution: _____

Phone: _____ Fax: _____

Address: _____

_____

E-mail: _____ Website: _____

Box number: _____

Key location: _____

Notes on steps to inventory and access contents: _____

_____

Savings Accounts

❑ There are no savings accounts.

❑ I have identified the following savings accounts and notified the institution of the death:

Name of institution: _____

Phone: _____ Fax: _____

Address: _____

_____

E-mail: _____ Website: _____

Account number: _____

Name of institution: _____

Phone: _____ Fax: _____

Address: _____

_____

E-mail: _____ Website: _____

Account number: _____

Name of institution: _____

Phone: _____ Fax: _____

Address: _____

_____

E-mail: _____ Website: _____

Account number: _____

Savings Bonds

❏   There are no savings bonds.

❏   I have identified the following savings bonds:

Series	Denomination	Serial Number	Issue Date

Banking: Other

Other miscellaneous information of interest:

_____

_____

_____

_____

_____

_____

_____

_____

_____

_____

_____

_____

_____

_____

_____

_____

_____

_____

_____

_____

_____

_____

_____

_____

_____

_____

_____

CHAPTER 6
LEARN WHAT'S AVAILABLE
IN INVESTMENTS

Your loved one may have invested money in any number of ways, such as by using an online trading account, relying on a financial advisor, or building a nest egg in mutual funds and certificates of deposit. There may be multiple types of investments that you will inherit and will need to continue to manage.

This chapter briefly covers some of the ways money can be invested, including stocks, bonds, and mutual funds. If you do inherit any investments, you'll need to know what types of investments are most appropriate for your circumstances. For example, your investment needs and objectives as a widow or widower may call for a different type of portfolio than you and your spouse had while you were a couple. You can use the checklists in this chapter to methodically identify investment accounts in your loved one's estate and check the rights of survivors to those investments.

You also need to determine if your loved one had any retirement savings accounts and understand what you need to do to claim the money in those funds as a surviving spouse or beneficiary. You also need to consider how to select the financial professionals who can help you along the way. Refer to Chapter 3 on selecting financial professionals.

My to-do checklist

Done   **Need to Do**

❏   ❏   Understand the different types of investments

❏   ❏   Get tax advice on how to take distribution of and manage any sums you inherit from a 401(k) or IRA

❏   ❏   Identify all investment accounts

❑ ❑ Promptly contact any investment professionals so that accounts can be valued as of the date of death for tax purposes

❑ ❑ Identify all retirement plans

❑ ❑ Contact all employers and former employers for information on any retirement savings accounts

❑ ❑ Search for any unclaimed money

❑ ❑ Complete the checklists for Chapter 6

Investment action checklists

The Action Checklists in Chapter 6 are set out in the following order:

- *Bonds*
- *Money Market Funds and Accounts*
- *Mutual Funds*
- *Stocks*
- *Individual Retirement Accounts (IRAs)*
- *Roth IRA*
- *401(k), 457(b), 403(b), and TSP Plans*
- *SIMPLE IRA*
- *SEP IRA*
- *Investments: Other*

✓ Understand the different types of investments

Stocks When you own a stock, you own part of a company. Companies sell these pieces of ownership, known as shares, to raise money to finance their businesses. When you buy a stock, you are betting that the company will grow. As the company does well, your stock generally increases in value. You can earn money on your investment either when the price of the stock rises or if the company shares company profits by paying a dividend. If the company does poorly, you can lose some of or all the money you paid for the share.

There are more than 3,000 companies listed on the New York Stock Exchange. Stocks are categorized in multiple ways, such as by industry (auto, biotechnology), by market sector (utilities, health care), or by geography (U.S., Asian). They can also be categorized by size, as in large-capitalization, or large-cap (generally companies worth more than $5 billion), mid-cap ($1 to $5 billion), or small-cap ($250 million to $1 billion). Another way to group stocks is based on financial experts' perception of the company's basic financial health and historical performance. These categories include growth stocks, value stocks, and income stocks. Knowing how a particular company's stocks are categorized helps you diversify your investments in different types of companies. Diversification reduces your risk of losing money.

Bonds When you buy a bond, you loan money to a company or government entity. The entity commits to paying you interest at a fixed rate for the life of the loan and to return to you the value of the loan by a certain date, called the maturity date. When you invest in a bond, you are taking the risk that the borrower may not be able to pay the interest or the principal. You also run the risk that if interest rates rise and you need to sell the bond, your bond may lose value because other investors can buy higher-rate bonds and thus you have to sell yours at a lower price to attract a buyer. If you buy a "callable" bond, the company has the right to pay you back before the maturity date, which is normally done when the company can borrow at a cheaper rate.

Bonds issued by the federal government are the safest investment vehicle to own. Treasury bills, notes, and bonds are available with maturities ranging from 1 to 30 years. They can be easily sold, but like all bonds, their values rise and fall as interest rates change. You pay no federal income tax on the interest you earn on these investments.

State and local governments also issue bonds to pay for things like roads, schools, and public safety. You pay no federal income tax on the interest and may not have to pay state taxes if you live in the area where the bond is issued. Because of this tax advantage, the interest rates on municipal bonds are lower than on other types of bonds.

Mutual Funds When you buy shares of a mutual fund, you own a bit of the various stocks, bonds, or other types of investments in the fund. Buying shares of a mutual fund helps you diversify because you are spreading the risk of losing your money among many different investments. Investments within a mutual fund are chosen by a professional manager based on the fund's investment objectives. The fund's objectives, set out in a public document called a prospectus, might be to own growth stock, own government bonds, or invest in a particular industry, such as pharmaceuticals.

Morningstar, a provider of mutual fund research, tracks more than 15,000 mutual funds, so you have many to choose from. Some of the common types of mutual funds are the following:

- Stock funds that invest in the stocks of many companies
- Bond funds that are a collection of bonds purchased with pooled money from many investors
- Money market funds that include short-term, low-risk loans
- Index funds that are made up of all the securities in a particular index, such as the Standard & Poor's 500 index
- Balanced funds that include a mix of stocks and bonds
- Life-cycle funds, or target retirement date funds, that are designed to increase the percentage of bonds in relation to stocks as the investor gets closer to retirement age or the specific target date

Money market accounts and money market funds have significant differences. A **money market account** is a type of savings account offered by a financial institution. Typically, the financial institution will pay a higher rate of interest than on regular savings accounts. You are able to make withdrawals at any time and can access the funds through automatic teller machines or by writing a check. As with other accounts in banks that are insured by the Federal Deposit Insurance Corporation, or FDIC, your money would be insured up to $250,000. You may have to maintain a minimum amount to avoid fees and may be restricted on how many withdrawals you can make in a month. A **money market fund**, on the other hand, is a type of mutual fund that is required by law to invest in low-risk, short-term debt. These funds are not insured.

As with any type of investment, you need to carefully match the fund's objectives with your own investment objectives. You also need to pay attention to the fund's fees. High fees or expense ratios can reduce your earnings.

Your personal and financial situation most likely has changed as a result of the death of your loved one. You may need access to cash to pay off debts, taxes, and funeral expenses. You may have significantly different needs for income and new investment objectives. Depending on your circumstances, you may have a large lump sum of money that you need to invest strategically as you may be facing the loss of the principal breadwinner in the family. There also can be important decisions that you need to make about taxes. If you have inherited an investment portfolio as a joint owner or a named beneficiary, at some point in the near future you'll want to sit down with a financial planner to go over the portfolio. It's wise to get expert counsel on these important financial matters.

Retirement Accounts Your loved one may have set up one or more accounts to save money for retirement and then to pay out income during retirement. With most retirement accounts, your loved one has most likely named a beneficiary or beneficiaries to receive the balance remaining in the fund or any death benefit.

Many employers have set up retirement savings plans into which a portion of the employee's salary is deposited each pay period. The employer may also "match" some of the employee's contributions to increase the amount invested. The employee can select how the contributions are invested by choosing from a variety of mutual funds. The employer-based funds are called **401(k) plans**, referring to a section of the Internal Revenue Service (IRS) code that allows contributions to be made before paying taxes on the amount of the contribution. Other similar plans with similar requirements are **457(b) plans** for state and local government employees and **403(b) plans** for religious, educational, and nonprofit organizations. Withdrawals are taxed when they are paid out.

✓ **Get tax advice on how to take distribution of and manage any sums you inherit from a 401(k) or an IRA**

You should be aware of some important rules so that you as a beneficiary can get the best tax advantages and avoid big tax hits if you don't handle the investment properly. Do not cash out the account until you've talked with a tax advisor about your options and the proper way to handle the account.

As a survivor, you should know that spouses are the automatic beneficiary of the 401(k) unless the spouse consented to another being named as the beneficiary. That waiver must be in writing. If no beneficiary is named, the account will be part of the decedent's estate.

Although the IRS sets out general rules for the distribution of 401(k) balances to spouses or named beneficiaries, not all 401(k) plans are the same. You will need to locate the plan documents for the specifics about how and when you need to receive the assets. Many plans may require you to take the money in a lump sum, on which you'll need to pay taxes. You won't have to pay the 10 percent penalty even if you or the decedent is under the age of 59½. If you are the spouse, you can roll the lump sum into an IRA, which means that you won't have to pay taxes until you start to make withdrawals from it. You should probably do a direct rollover, which means that the 401(k) plan will directly transfer the money to the financial institution that holds your IRA. Otherwise, if you don't deposit the lump-sum check within 60 days into an IRA, you lose the tax benefit and will have to pay taxes on the full amount. Some plans may allow you to stretch out the payments and thereby delay paying the taxes, especially if the decedent was already receiving periodic payments when he or she died. You will have to check with the plan administrator to see what your options are for electing a different payment plan. Because there are serious tax implications, you need to get advice from a tax advisor.

Another type of retirement savings account is an individual retirement account or **IRA**. An IRA can be set up at the place of employer or as a separate investment account. As with 401(k) accounts, money placed in an IRA grows tax free until withdrawals are made. In additional to a traditional IRA, there are other types of accounts. A **SIMPLE IRA**, or Savings Incentive Math Plan for Employees, is for employees of small companies or the self-employed. As with traditional IRAs, the employee can select from a variety of invest-ment options within the plan.

A **SEP IRA**, or Simplified Employer Pension, is another way business owners can provide retirement savings plans for themselves and their employees. With a **Roth IRA**, the tax benefits are switched. Taxes are paid on the money placed into the Roth, but with-drawals are tax free.

When a spouse inherits an IRA, he or she can either retitle the IRA into his or her own name or roll the IRA—tax free—into an IRA he or she owns. As a spouse, you will then need to follow the rules about IRA withdrawals: no tax penalty if you withdraw money after age 59½, mandatory withdrawals when you reach 70½. If you are younger than 59½ and want to have access to the money in the IRA without a 10 percent tax penalty, you'll need to retitle the IRA as an "inherited" IRA. Done properly, you can make withdrawals pen-alty free. After age 59½, you will need to again retitle the IRA so that you can delay your mandatory withdrawals until you reach 70½ rather than when your deceased spouse would have reached 70½. Again, get advice from a professional because the titling can be tricky!

If you are a nonspouse beneficiary, you have two options. You can take distributions over your life expectancy, or you must liquidate the account within five years of the death of the original owner and pay the taxes. The first option, called a stretch IRA, lets you allow the money to grow tax free over a much longer time before you have to pay taxes on the investment. You do, however, need to take some distributions by December 31 of the year following the year of the original owner's death. If you miss that first distribution, you have to take all the funds out within five years. With a Roth IRA, the distributions are tax free as long as the IRA is at least five years old.

If no beneficiary is named on an IRA, the account is paid to the estate and the beneficiary must follow the five-year rule for distributions.

✓ Identify all investment accounts

Ideally, your loved one kept meticulous records of all investments neatly and conveniently organized so that you can readily identify all accounts and financial advisors. If that isn't quite the circumstance, here are some suggestions.

- Look for periodic statements that indicate the account number and contact information.

- Watch the mail or e-mail for any letters, notices, or a prospectus that would identify where accounts might be located.

- Check checkbooks or bank account statements to look for payments or deposits to an investment account or for interest or dividend credits from investments.

- Check safe-deposit boxes for stock certificates, bonds, or certificates of deposit. Refer to Chapter 5 for information on how to access and inventory safe-deposit boxes.

- Examine income tax returns for income from investments.

- Look on contact lists for the names of accountants, insurance agents, investment advisors, or financial planners who would have information about investments.

✓ Promptly contact any investment professionals so that accounts can be valued as of the date of death for tax purposes

Once you have identified any investment accounts, you will need to contact the company, financial institution, or financial professional holding the investment. You'll need a copy of the death certificate, documentation of your authority to act on behalf of your family member (such as your letters of appointment from the probate court), and the account information. What happens next depends on the type of the investment and how the investment was owned.

✓ Identify all retirement plans

The place to start looking for employer-based retirement savings accounts, or 401(k)s, is with the current employer and any former employers. Start with the human relations department for information about how to contact the plan administrator and get a copy of the plan rules. Look for monthly or quarterly statements of contributions. If your loved one was already receiving distributions from the plan, look for account statements, bank account entries for deposits, or income tax returns that would identify the plan administrator.

✓ Contact all employers and former employers for information on any retirement savings accounts

IRAs, as "individual" retirement accounts, can show up in many places. A person may have more than one IRA that he or she set up for different investment purposes, and they may be housed in different institutions. Here again, old tax returns may indicate contributions or distributions. The human relations department at past employers may show where roll-over contributions were sent. Check with any financial advisors who may have records that inventory various assets.

✓ Search for unclaimed money

One place to go to look for "forgotten" money is the website of the National Association of Unclaimed Property Administrators at www.missingmoney.com. Under most state laws, money held by financial institutions and insurance companies, and even a tax refund that goes unclaimed for a number of years, must be turned over to a state agency for safekeeping until the money is claimed. At this website, you will find a database of governmental unclaimed property that you can search for free.

Investments Checklists

Bonds

❏   There are no bonds or bond funds.

❏   I have identified the following bonds or bond funds and notified the institution holding these bonds of the death:

Name of institution: _____

Phone: _____ Fax: _____

Address: _____

_____

E-mail: _____ Website: _____

Account number: _____

Name of institution: _____

Phone: _____ Fax: _____

Address: _____

_____

E-mail: _____ Website: _____

Account number: _____

Name of institution: _____

Phone: _____ Fax: _____

Address: _____

_____

E-mail: _____ Website: _____

Account number: _____

Money Market Funds and Accounts

- ❏ There are no money market funds.

- ❏ I have identified the following money market funds and notified the institution holding these funds of the death:

Name of institution: _____

Phone: _____ Fax: _____

Address: _____

_____

E-mail: _____ Website: _____

Account number: _____

Name of institution: _____

Phone: _____ Fax: _____

Address: _____

_____

E-mail: _____ Website: _____

Account number: _____

- ❏ There are no money market accounts.

- ❏ I have identified the following money market accounts and notified the institution holding these accounts of the death:

Name of institution: _____

Phone: _____ Fax: _____

Address: _____

_____

E-mail: _____ Website: _____

Account number: _____

Mutual Funds

❑ There are no mutual funds.

❑ I have identified the following mutual funds and notified the institution holding these funds of the death:

Name of institution: _____

Phone: _____ Fax: _____

Address: _____

_____

E-mail: _____ Website: _____

Account number: _____

Name of institution: _____

Phone: _____ Fax: _____

Address: _____

_____

E-mail: _____ Website: _____

Account number: _____

Name of institution: _____

Phone: _____ Fax: _____

Address: _____

_____

E-mail: _____ Website: _____

Account number: _____

Stocks

❑   There are no stocks.

❑   I have identified the following stocks and notified the institution holding these stocks of the death:

Name of institution: _____

Phone: _____ Fax: _____

Address: _____

_____

E-mail: _____ Website: _____

Account number: _____

Name of institution: _____

Phone: _____ Fax: _____

Address: _____

_____

E-mail: _____ Website: _____

Account number: _____

Name of institution: _____

Phone: _____ Fax: _____

Address: _____

_____

E-mail: _____ Website: _____

Account number: _____

Individual Retirement Accounts (IRAs)

- ❏ There are no IRAs.
- ❏ I have identified the following IRAs and notified the custodian of these accounts of the death.
- ❏ I have delivered the death certificate.
- ❏ There are benefits to survivors under this plan.
- ❏ There are no benefits to survivors under this plan.

Name of custodian: _____

Phone: _____ Fax: _____

Address: _____

_____

E-mail: _____ Website: _____

Account number: _____

Name of custodian: _____

Phone: _____ Fax: _____

Address: _____

_____

E-mail: _____ Website: _____

Account number: _____

Name of custodian: _____

Phone: _____ Fax: _____

Address: _____

_____

E-mail: _____ Website: _____

Account number: _____

Roth IRA

- ❏ There are no Roth IRAs.
- ❏ I have identified the following Roth IRAs and notified the custodian of these accounts of the death.
- ❏ I have delivered a copy of the death certificate.
- ❏ There are benefits to survivors under this plan.
- ❏ There are no benefits to survivors under this plan.

Name of custodian: _____

Phone: _____ Fax: _____

Address: _____

_____

E-mail: _____ Website: _____

Account number: _____

Name of custodian: _____

Phone: _____ Fax: _____

Address: _____

_____

E-mail: _____ Website: _____

Account number: _____

Name of custodian: _____

Phone: _____ Fax: _____

Address: _____

_____

E-mail: _____ Website: _____

Account number: _____

401(k), 457(b), 403(b), and TSP Plans

❑ There are no retirement savings plans (401(k)).

❑ There are no state or local government employee retirement savings plans (457(b)).

❑ There are no religious, educational, or non-profit organization employee retirement savings plans (403(b)).

❑ There is no federal employee Thrift Savings Plan (TSP).

❑ I have identified the following 401(k), 457(b), 403(b), or TSP plans and notified the plan administrator of the death.

❑ I have delivered a copy of the death certificate.

❑ There are benefits to survivors under this plan.

❑ There are no benefits to survivors under this plan.

Name of administrator: _____

Phone: _____ Fax: _____

Address: _____

_____

E-mail: _____ Website: _____

Account number: _____

Name of administrator: _____

Phone: _____ Fax: _____

Address: _____

_____

E-mail: _____ Website: _____

Account number: _____

Name of administrator: _____

Phone: _____ Fax: _____

Address: _____

_____

E-mail: _____ Website: _____

Account number: _____

SIMPLE IRA

❑   There are no SIMPLE (Savings Incentive Math Plan for Employees) IRAs.

❑   I have identified the following SIMPLE IRAs and notified the custodian of the death.

❑   I have delivered a copy of the death certificate.

❑   There are benefits to survivors under this plan.

❑   There are no benefits to survivors under this plan.

Name of custodian: _____

Phone: _____ Fax: _____

Address: _____

_____

E-mail: _____ Website: _____

Account number: _____

Name of custodian: _____

Phone: _____ Fax: _____

Address: _____

_____

E-mail: _____ Website: _____

Account number: _____

Name of custodian: _____

Phone: _____ Fax: _____

Address: _____

_____

E-mail: _____ Website: _____

Account number: _____

SEP IRA

- ❏ There are no SEP (Simplified Employer Pension) IRAs.
- ❏ I have identified the following SEP IRAs and notified the custodian of the death.
- ❏ I have delivered a copy of the death certificate.
- ❏ There are benefits to survivors under this plan.
- ❏ There are no benefits to survivors under this plan.

Name of custodian: _____

Phone: _____ Fax: _____

Address: _____

_____

E-mail: _____ Website: _____

Account number: _____

Name of custodian: _____

Phone: _____ Fax: _____

Address: _____

_____

E-mail: _____ Website: _____

Account number: _____

Name of custodian: _____

Phone: _____ Fax: _____

Address: _____

_____

E-mail: _____ Website: _____

Account number: _____

Investments: Other

Other miscellaneous information of interest:

_____

_____

_____

_____

_____

_____

_____

_____

_____

_____

_____

_____

_____

_____

_____

_____

_____

_____

_____

_____

_____

_____

_____

_____

_____

_____

_____

_____

_____

_____

_____

_____

_____

_____

_____

CHAPTER 7
CHECK ON INSURANCE BENEFITS

Insurance offers a way to spread the risk of a financial loss among many people. The payment of annual premiums protects the insured (up to the limits of the policy) against losses from the death or disability of the family breadwinner, fire, theft, accident, or liability, depending on the type of insurance purchased. Any loss is shared by all those insured, saving the individual from financial disaster. In other words, the group absorbs the individual's unexpected losses.

Because of the death of your family member, you may be entitled to insurance proceeds or protections. You may have to file insurance claims to receive proceeds due to you, cancel certain policies, or obtain new policies in order to protect your loved one's property. To be able to take advantage of the insurance that your loved one obtained to protect your family and property, you need to know about all the different types of insurance policies.

An amazing number of life insurance proceeds go unclaimed because the policyholder's family or heirs didn't know about them. Use the checklists in this chapter to identify all the possible policies and record the names and addresses of the agents and companies you need to contact.

My to-do checklist

Done	Need to Do	
❑	❑	Review terms of all life insurance policies
❑	❑	Locate all insurance policies (life, care, homeowners, etc.)
❑	❑	Contact the insurance company for instructions on how to file a claim for annuity or life insurance benefits
❑	❑	Determine your health insurance options
❑	❑	Get help paying Medicare costs
❑	❑	Notify any health insurance plans

❑   ❑   Notify the vehicle insurance company so that there is complete coverage until the vehicle is sold or transferred

❑   ❑   Contact the insurance company to ensure that the home and its contents are properly insured

❑   ❑   Make sure that a homeowners' or renters' policy remains in effect if no one is going to be living in the home

❑   ❑   Complete the checklists for Chapter 7

Insurance action checklists

The Action Checklists in Chapter 7 are set out in the following order:

- *Annuities*
- *Automobile Insurance*
- *Health, Disability, and Medicare Health Insurance*
- *Homeowners' Insurance*
- *Life Insurance*
- *Other Residence Insurance*
- *Other Vehicle Insurance*
- *Insurance: Other*

The following descriptions are not a detailed breakdown of the many types of insurance options available. They should, however, give you some information about the most widely used types of insurance coverage to help you locate all insurance benefits available to you and your family.

✓ Review terms of all life insurance policies

Life insurance is primarily intended to ease the financial loss to a beneficiary that results from the policyholder's death. Although death comes to everyone and cannot be considered "unexpected" in the long run, it can certainly be unexpected when it occurs. Life insurance is a way to make sure that you and other surviving family members have cash to pay for the loved one's final expenses, such as final medical expenses or a funeral. A life insurance policy can also be used to provide cash for any estate taxes or unpaid debts. Life insurance also may be important to provide the financial support that you and your children will need after your spouse's death.

Today's life insurance market has multiple options to choose from, including how much coverage to purchase, the size of the premiums, how the policy is invested, any guarantees on returns, and how and when the policy proceeds are paid out to the beneficiaries.

A life insurance policy pays a designated sum of money to the person the policyholder named as the beneficiary to receive the policy proceeds on the death of the insured person. The beneficiary can be the insured's estate, or it can be one or more individuals. This money may be paid in a lump sum, in a monthly sum for the life of another individual, in monthly sums over a certain length of time, or in some other manner spelled out by the terms of the policy. The amount you will receive as a beneficiary is set out in the policy. A so-called **double indemnity** policy may even pay twice as much if your loved one's death is caused by an accident.

A widely purchased form of life insurance is **whole life insurance**. This type of insurance pays a sum of money (the "face value") to the named beneficiary at the time of the policyholder's death, if all premiums have been paid to keep the insurance in force. **Universal life**, **variable whole life**, and **variable universal life** are different types of permanent life insurance in which the policyholder has the option to vary (within the terms of the contract) the amount paid in premiums from year to year and how the policy's cash reserves grow. Typically, the cash value reserves held by the insurance company are invested in stocks, bonds, or mutual funds. The policyholder selects the investments from a menu offered by the insurance company. Some policies have guaranteed minimum returns on the investment; others allow the policyholder to borrow against the cash value of the policy. How much you will receive as a beneficiary varies based on many factors, including the terms of the policy, the amounts paid in premiums, and the investment success of the insurance company.

Term insurance, on the other hand, provides insurance coverage only for a specified length of time, such as 5 years, 10 years, or 20 years. The annual premium for term insurance is substantially less than the annual premium for whole life insurance. Many term life insurance contracts provide that the policy may be renewed at the end of the term or be converted to a permanent type of life insurance without providing further proof of insurability. If you are the named beneficiary of the policy and the policy has not expired, you'll receive the death benefit. If the policy term has expired, you'll have no claim.

Annuities are a type of life insurance that is typically designed to provide a stream of income. As with other types of insurance, there are many types of annuities. They may be fixed, variable, or indexed, depending on how the principal is invested, and may have immediate or deferred payments, depending on when payouts are made. Typically, money invested in an annuity grows tax-deferred, with payouts being taxed as the return of principal and ordinary income.

The policyholder has many options as to how to invest the money within the annuity, at what point the annuity begins to make payments, and for how long and to whom payments will be made. Payouts may be made for a fixed number of years, or during the policyholder's lifetime, or for the lifetime of a spouse or other beneficiary. For an additional cost, the policyholder can also obtain specific benefits, such as a guaranteed minimum death benefit (GMDB) or a guaranteed minimum withdrawal benefit (GMWB). A GMDB means that the named beneficiaries or the policyholder's estate will receive a set amount as defined in the contract if the policyholder dies before the annuity begins paying benefits. A GMWB means that the policyholder while alive will receive a fixed percentage of the investment each year. Be certain that you understand the terms of any annuity your loved one has and what you need to do as a survivor or beneficiary of the annuity.

✓ Locate all insurance policies (life, car, homeowners, etc.)

As a survivor, you'll have to track down all annuity and life insurance policies. Some companies may require that you hand over the original life insurance policies before you can collect any proceeds. In any event, you have to go to the insurance company with documentation that you are entitled to the proceeds; they won't come looking for you.

If your loved one's paperwork was organized, each life insurance policy should be readily accessible. If that is not the case, you'll need to do some detective work to be sure you have located all policies. You don't want to overlook any policies.

- Many employers provide group life insurance for their employees, and partnerships often fund buy-sell agreements with life insurance. Be sure to check at the last places of employment for any work-related insurance policies.

- Check the last several years of income tax returns. Some life insurance policies pay annual dividends. A listing of income from an insurance company is a lead you need to follow.

- Go through old bank statements, canceled checks, and credit card statements to look for premium payments to an insurance company.

- Watch for a premium notice to come in the mail.

- Look in files, safe-deposit boxes, and drawers for policies. Look in address books or contact lists for names of insurance agents.

- The National Association of Insurance Commissioners has an online tool at https://eapps.naic.org/orphanedpolicy/ that can help you find state insurance departments that may be able to help you in your search.

- The National Association of Unclaimed Property Administrators offers a Missing Money.com website where you can conduct a free online national search for unclaimed money held by state authorities, including life insurance policies. You'll be successful only if the policy has been deemed unclaimed after a number of years and transferred to the state.

- The MIB Group at www.mib.com/lost_life_insurance.html maintains a database of life insurance applications going back to 1996. If you are an executor, surviving spouse, or close relative, you can request a record search through MIB's policy locator service for $75. The search won't tell you what policies have been purchased, but you will know at which companies applications for policies have been made.

- Check with the deceased's attorney, financial advisor, and insurance agent to learn what they know about any policies. The agent who sold the car insurance may also have sold life insurance.

✓ Contact the insurance company for instructions on how to file a claim for annuity or life insurance benefits

Once you have located any annuity or life insurance policies, you will need to contact that company for instructions on how you can file a claim. Although the steps you need to take will vary depending on the company, you will most likely need copies of the death certificate and proof of your relationship, such as a marriage license or birth certificate.

Insurance companies sometimes merge or change their names, making it difficult to know how to contact a company to file a claim. The National Association of Insurance Commissioners' website at www.naic.org/consumer_life_co_locator.htm can help you locate insurance companies.

✓ Determine your health insurance options

Health insurance provides a means to pay doctor, hospital, and other medical expenses if you become sick or are in an accident. Most people get health insurance as an employee benefit where they work. Some people can continue to get health coverage through their former employer's health plan after they retire. Employers don't have to provide retiree health insurance, and they can cut or eliminate those benefits. Most employee policies allow for coverage of family members, generally for an additional premium. Whether the retiree can cover family members depends on the plan. If you have been covered under your loved one's group plan for employees or for retirees, you need to contact the employer's benefit coordinator to determine whether or for how long you will continue to be covered after your loved one's death.

If you and your family had health insurance through your spouse's employment, you should be entitled to continue that coverage, but you will have to pay 100 percent of the premiums. In other words, you will need to pay the employer's share of the premiums in addition to the premiums your spouse was already paying. Your access to continued coverage, called COBRA coverage, lasts for 18 months, unless the plan or your state allows a longer period. You must notify the employer within 30 days of the death. You then have 60 days in which to decide if you want to take the COBRA coverage and 45 more days to make your initial premium payment. The employer's benefit manager can give you more details about this continued coverage.

Although COBRA premiums will be high, they may be more affordable than individual policies. Before purchasing any type of health insurance, be certain that you understand what is and is not covered. Many different types of accident and illness insurance policies exist. Some are very limited in scope and pay out only if the policyholder developed a specific type of illness, such as cancer. Other policies, however, provide very broad coverage, although each has its limitations.

Medical expense reimbursement policies range from a policy that pays $10 for each day you are hospitalized to health insurance policies that cover almost every medical expense the policyholder could encounter. Because the coverage varies to such a great extent, the cost of medical and accident coverage varies greatly.

Health Insurance Marketplace If you need to purchase insurance and are not yet eligible for Medicare, you can shop for and purchase insurance in the Health Insurance Marketplace in your state. This new way to obtain health insurance allows you to compare the benefits and costs of approved private health plans side by side. All health plans sold in the Marketplace must cover basic health benefits, including doctor visits, hospitalization, medical care, mental health services, and prescription drugs. When shopping for insurance in the Marketplace, you can pick from several levels of coverage, which will allow you to find a plan that works best for you and your budget. Depending on your income, you may be able to get financial assistance to pay your premiums. If you are eligible for insurance through a Marketplace and do not buy any insurance, you will be subject to a penalty. Go to www.healthcare.gov to compare available plans and sign up for coverage.

Medicare Medicare is a federal health insurance program for people who are age 65 and over, for some younger people with disabilities, and for people with end-stage kidney disease. Medicare does not cover dependents or spouses under the age of 65.

The Medicare program has several parts. **Part A** helps pay for inpatient hospital care as well as some home health care, preventive screenings, hospice care, and limited skilled nursing care. You do not have to pay any premiums for Part A coverage because you have already paid for it through your payroll taxes.

Part B helps pay for doctor visits, some home health care, medical equipment, some preventive services, outpatient hospital care, rehabilitative therapy, laboratory tests, X-rays, mental health services, ambulance services, and blood transfusions. When you turn 65, you are automatically signed up for Part A and Part B if you are receiving Social Security or Railroad Retirement benefits. You do have to pay a premium ($104.90 in 2013) for Part B. You can decline Part B if you are covered by another policy. You can later sign up for Part B if your employer or retiree coverage ends, but you have only a short time to apply for Part B. If you wait too long, you will have to pay more in premiums.

Part C is now known as Medicare Advantage. Medicare Advantage plans are offered by private companies that have been approved by Medicare to offer this type of coverage. You have the option of purchasing Medicare Advantage coverage once you have enrolled in Parts A and B. These policies pay for the same services as Parts A and B and may offer other benefits such as dental, vision, and prescription drug coverage. In most Medicare Advantage plans, you can go only to doctors, specialists, and hospitals that are on the plan's list. During open enrollment periods between October and December of each year, you can change Medicare Advantage plans or select traditional Medicare (Part A and Part B).

Part D helps pay for prescription drugs. You have the option of purchasing prescription drug coverage through private insurance companies that have been approved by

Medicare to sell this type of insurance. You can choose from many drug plans offered by many companies. The benefits and costs vary between insurance companies and each company's several plans. You can elect to purchase Part D drug coverage when you are newly eligible for Medicare. If you wait, you will have to pay a late enrollment penalty. Each year, you can switch drug plans during the open enrollment period from October to December.

Medicare doesn't pay for all health care costs. People with Medicare are responsible for an annual deductible, coinsurance, or copayments. Medicare also does not pay for long-term care. You may want to consider purchasing Medicare supplemental insurance, also called **Medigap** insurance. Medigap insurance covers some of the costs that Medicare does not pay. This private health insurance is offered by Medicare-approved insurance companies, and each company can offer up to 11 standardized plans. These standard plans are labeled Plans A through N, although plans E, H, I, and J are no longer available to new purchasers. Each standard plan offers a different set of benefits, fills different gaps in Medicare coverage, and varies in price. For example, the benefits covered in one company's "Plan G" would be the same as those covered by another company's Plan G, but the price each company charges can be different. The standardization of plans helps you more easily compare policies among companies.

You can compare the various Medicare plans, including prescription drug, Medigap, and Medicare Advantage, at www.medicare.gov/find-a-plan. For a complete guide to Medicare, see AARP's *Medicare for Dummies* by Patricia Barry at www.aarp.org /MedicareForDummies.

✓ Get help paying Medicare costs

If you are eligible, you may want to take advantage of state programs that help pay for the medical expenses not covered by Medicare. States have programs that pay Medicare premiums—and, in some cases, the Part A and Part B copayments, coinsurance, and deductibles—for people with Medicare coverage who have limited income and resources. In general, you need to have Part A and an annual income less than $13,788 for an individual and resources less than $7,080 (in 2013). These amounts and the eligibility requirements vary from state to state and year to year. You need to check with your state Medicaid office for the details of the various Medicare Savings Programs available in your state. Some states are able to provide help to people with higher income levels, and others don't have any limits on resources. Resources include money in checking and savings accounts, stocks, bonds, mutual funds, and individual retirement accounts (IRAs). Resources that don't count toward the resource limit include a home, car, burial plot, burial expenses up to your state's limit, furniture, and other household items.

A program called Extra Help can reduce your prescription drug costs if your income is less than $17,235 and your resources are less than $13,300 (in 2013). If you qualify and join a Medicare Part D prescription drug plan, you'll get help paying your drug plan's premiums, deductible, coinsurance, and copayments. You are automatically eligible for Extra Help if you get help from your state Medicaid programs paying your Part B premiums or you get Supplemental Security Income benefits. If you don't automatically qualify for Extra Help, you can apply online at www.socialsecurity.gov/i1020, call Social Security at 1-800-772-1213 to apply by phone, or visit your state Medicaid office.

Medicaid is a joint federal and state program that can also help you with your medical costs if you have low income and resources. People who qualify for both Medicare and Medicaid are called "dual eligibles." Medicaid programs vary from state to state and have different income and resources requirements, so you need to call your state Medicaid office to find out if you are eligible.

Some states have **State Pharmacy Assistance Programs** (SPAP) that can help people pay for their prescription drugs based on financial need, age, or medical condition. Many major drug manufacturers also have **Pharmaceutical Assistance Programs** (PAP) to help people pay for their medications. Visit http://www.medicare.gov/pharmaceutical -assistance-program/index.aspx to find out if any of the drugs you are taking are covered by any PAP.

To find out about other programs that may be available in your state to help with your medical expenses, contact your **State Health Insurance Assistance Program** (SHIP). SHIP counselors can tell you what programs you are eligible for and help you apply. You can find the phone number for your local SHIP at www.shiptalk.org or by calling the Elder Care Locator at 1-800-677-1166.

✓ Notify any health insurance plans

If your loved one was on Medicare, you need to promptly notify the Social Security Administration at 1-800-772-1213 (TTY: 1-800-325-0778). You should also notify any Medicare Advantage, Part D prescription drug plan, or Medicare supplemental plan administrator. You should find that contact information on any recent statement.

✓ Notify the vehicle insurance company so that there is complete coverage until the vehicle is sold or transferred

Automobile insurance is usually a necessity for any owner of a motor vehicle. In fact, many states require all drivers to be insured for liability to other persons for damages resulting from an automobile accident. Regardless of the law in your particular state, you need to make sure that any vehicle your loved one owned remains insured until you transfer title to someone else or until you sell it. The executor or administrator of the estate should notify the insurance company and ask to be added as the owner of the vehicle insurance policy. You should also check to make sure that any RVs, motorcycles, boats, snowmobiles, and other vehicles are insured.

✓ **Contact the insurance company to ensure that the home and its contents are properly insured**

You also need to check to make sure that the home and all its contents are adequately insured. If you as a co-owner of the house are going to continue to live in the home, you most likely do not need to make any changes to the policy, but you should notify the insurance company of the death of your loved one. The executor or administrator of the estate should ask to be placed on the policy as a named insured. Doing so will make sure that the executor has all the same protections and rights under the policy as did the deceased.

Any new owner who inherits the house must notify the insurance company to ensure that any claims the new owner has to make will be covered. Carefully read the existing policy to see how long the original policy will remain in effect after the homeowner's death. It may be only a couple of months, so act quickly to set up the new policy in the new owner's name. You don't want to be in the expensive position of having a claim denied or the policy declared void because the correct name doesn't appear on the policy.

✓ **Make sure that a homeowners' or renters' policy remains in effect if no one is going to be living in the home**

If the house is going to be vacant for an extended time, let's say more than a month, you definitely need to notify the insurance company to make sure that the policy remains in effect. You may need to purchase additional insurance for the time being until the house is sold or occupied. The insurance company may require assurance that someone periodically checks on the vacant house to prevent vandalism or frozen pipes. Even if you are planning to sell the home, you want to get confirmation in writing from the insurance company that coverage is in place until it is sold.

Use this sample letter to notify insurance companies of the death. Send two originals and ask that a signed original be returned to you as proof of the change in policy. Once again, a copy of the death certificate will need to be attached.

Sample Letter

Notice to Deceased's Homeowners' Insurance Company

Date: _____

_____

_____

_____

[insert insurance company name and address]

Name of deceased: _____

Deceased's address: _____

_____

Date of death: _____

Homeowners' insurance policy number: _____

This letter is to notify you that your insured, _____ *[deceased's name]*, died on _____ *[date of death]*. As the executor [or personal representative, *select appropriate title*] of the estate, I would like to be added as a named insured to this homeowners' insurance policy.

Enclosed with this letter you will find a certified death certificate for _____ *[deceased's name]* along with documentation that I am the [executor, *fill in appropriate title*].

Please contact me so that we may discuss this matter. I can be reached using the information below. Please sign and return the second copy of this letter in the enclosed stamped and self-addressed envelope.

Thank you for your assistance.

Signature: _____

Printed or typed name: _____

Relationship to deceased: _____

Address: _____

_____

Home phone: _____ Work phone: _____

E-mail: _____

Receipt acknowledged by

Signature: _____

Printed or typed name: _____

Title: _____

Date: _____

Enclosures:

Death certificate

Letter of probate administration appointment

Copy of letter

Self-addressed envelope

Insurance Action Checklists

Annuities

- ❑ There is no annuity.
- ❑ I have located the following annuity policies and companies.
- ❑ I have delivered a copy of the death certificate and proof of my relationship with the deceased.

Insurance company: _____

Agent: _____

Phone: _____ Fax: _____

Address: _____

_____

E-mail: _____ Website: _____

Policy number: _____

Terms: _____

Beneficiary/beneficiaries: _____

Insurance company: _____

Agent: _____

Phone: _____ Fax: _____

Address: _____

_____

E-mail: _____ Website: _____

Policy number: _____

Terms: _____

Beneficiary/beneficiaries: _____

Automobile Insurance

❏ There are no automobiles needing insurance coverage.

❏ I have identified the following automobile insurance coverage on the following vehicles and notified the company of the death:

Vehicle: _____

Year purchased: _____ Purchase price: _____

Insurance company: _____

Agent: _____

Phone: _____ Fax: _____

Address: _____

_____

E-mail: _____ Website: _____

Policy number: _____

Vehicle: _____

Year purchased: _____ Purchase price: _____

Insurance company: _____

Agent: _____

Phone: _____ Fax: _____

Address: _____

_____

E-mail: _____ Website: _____

Policy number: _____

Vehicle: _____

Year purchased: _____ Purchase price: _____

Insurance company: _____

Agent: _____

Phone: _____ Fax: _____

Address: _____

_____

E-mail: _____ Website: _____

Policy number: _____

Vehicle: _____

Year purchased: _____ Purchase price: _____

Insurance company: _____

Agent: _____

Phone: _____ Fax: _____

Address: _____

_____

E-mail: _____ Website: _____

Policy number: _____

Health, Disability, and Medicare Health Insurance

❏ I have identified the following health insurance policies or coverage carried by my loved one and notified the company of the death:

❏ Dental

❏ Disability

❏ Hospitalization

❏ Long-term care

❏ Major medical

❏ Medicare

❏ Medicare Advantage

❏ Medicare Supplemental Insurance (Medigap)

❏ Medicare Part D Prescription Drug Insurance

❏ Surgical

❏ Travel accidental death

❏ Vision

❏ Other: _____

❏ I have identified the following health insurance for myself:

❏ Dental

❏ Disability

❏ Hospitalization

❏ Long-term care

❏ Major medical

❏ Medicare

❏ Medicare Advantage

❏ Medicare Supplemental Insurance (Medigap)

❏ Medicare Part D Prescription Drug Insurance

❏ Surgical

❏ Travel accidental death

❏ Vision

❏ Other: _____

Insurance company: _____

Type of policy: _____

Agent: _____

Phone: _____ Fax: _____

Address: _____

_____

E-mail: _____ Website: _____

Policy number: _____

Group number: _____

Insurance company: _____

Type of policy: _____

Agent: _____

Phone: _____ Fax: _____

Address: _____

_____

E-mail: _____ Website: _____

Policy number: _____

Group number: _____

Insurance company: _____

Type of policy: _____

Agent: _____

Phone: _____ Fax: _____

Address: _____

_____

E-mail: _____ Website: _____

Policy number: _____

Group number: _____

Insurance company: _____

Type of policy: _____

Agent: _____

Phone: _____ Fax: _____

Address: _____

_____

E-mail: _____ Website: _____

Policy number: _____

Group number: _____

Insurance company: _____

Type of policy: _____

Agent: _____

Phone: _____ Fax: _____

Address: _____

_____

E-mail: _____ Website: _____

Policy number: _____

Group number: _____

Homeowners' Insurance

❑   There is no homeowners' or residence insurance.

❑   There is no renters' insurance.

❑   I have identified the following renters', homeowners', or residence insurance with the following companies and notified them of the death:

Insurance company: _____

Agent: _____

Phone: _____ Fax: _____

Address: _____

_____

E-mail: _____ Website: _____

Policy number: _____

Description of coverage: _____

Insurance company: _____

Agent: _____

Phone: _____ Fax: _____

Address: _____

_____

E-mail: _____ Website: _____

Policy number: _____

Description of coverage: _____

Life Insurance

❏ There is no life insurance policy.

❏ I have identified the following life insurance policies and notified the company of the death:

Insurance company: _____

Agent: _____

Phone: _____ Fax: _____

Address: _____

_____

E-mail: _____ Website: _____

Policy number: _____

Face amount: _____

Beneficiary/beneficiaries: _____

Insurance company: _____

Agent: _____

Phone: _____ Fax: _____

Address: _____

_____

E-mail: _____ Website: _____

Policy number: _____

Face amount: _____

Beneficiary/beneficiaries: _____

Other Residence Insurance

❑   There is no other residence.

❑   I have identified the following homeowners' or residence insurance on a second residence and notified the company of the death:

Insurance company: _____

Residence location: _____

Agent: _____

Phone: _____ Fax: _____

Address: _____

_____

E-mail: _____ Website: _____

Policy number: _____

Description of coverage: _____

Insurance company: _____

Residence location: _____

Agent: _____

Phone: _____ Fax: _____

Address: _____

_____

E-mail: _____ Website: _____

Policy number: _____

Description of coverage: _____

Other Vehicle Insurance

❑ There are no other vehicles to be insured, such as airplanes, boats, motorcycles, recreational vehicles, or snowmobiles.

❑ I have identified the following vehicles and notified the insurance company of the death:

Vehicle: _____

Year purchased: _____ Purchase price: _____

Insurance company: _____

Agent: _____

Phone: _____ Fax: _____

Address: _____

_____

E-mail: _____ Website: _____

Policy number: _____

Vehicle: _____

Year purchased: _____ Purchase price: _____

Insurance company: _____

Agent: _____

Phone: _____ Fax: _____

Address: _____

_____

E-mail: _____ Website: _____

Policy number: _____

Vehicle: _____

Year purchased: _____ Purchase price: _____

Insurance company: _____

Agent: _____

Phone: _____ Fax: _____

Address: _____

_____

E-mail: _____ Website: _____

Policy number: _____

Insurance: Other

Other miscellaneous information of interest:

_____

_____

_____

_____

_____

_____

_____

_____

_____

_____

_____

_____

_____

_____

_____

_____

_____

_____

_____

_____

_____

_____

_____

_____

_____

_____

_____

_____

_____

_____

_____

_____

CHAPTER 8

STAY PUT IN YOUR HOME FOR NOW

What happens to your home when your loved one dies can be a very critical issue. Will you be able to stay put for now and not have the additional disruption to your life of having to move? Will you continue as the owner of the home, or will someone else inherit the property? If there is no surviving spouse living in the home, family members may wonder what is going to happen to the residence. What needs to be considered if the home is in a condominium? What about other property such as a second home in another state or rental property? What happens to any property interest in a time-share?

Because real estate can take many forms, you first have to make sure that you understand how the home or other property is owned. How the property is titled makes a big difference in what happens next.

My to-do checklist

Done	Need to Do	
❑	❑	Secure all property for safety
❑	❑	Assemble copies of the deeds or other documentation of ownership to all real estate
❑	❑	Obtain a copy of the condominium's master deed and association documents
❑	❑	Review how the property is titled
❑	❑	Obtain a copy of any trust documents
❑	❑	Obtain a copy of any time-share contracts
❑	❑	Consult with an attorney about the need to change the title to any property if you are a surviving joint owner
❑	❑	Check out the rental agreement

❑　　　❑　　　Stay put for now

❑　　　❑　　　Complete the checklists for Chapter 8

Stay put action checklists

The Action Checklists in Chapter 8 are set out in the following order:

- *Commercial or Rental Property*
- *Condominium*
- *Farmland*
- *Rental Agreements*
- *Residence*
- *Time-share*
- *Real Estate: Other*

✓　Secure all property for safety

You need to make sure that the property is secure and safe, especially if no one is currently residing there. Thieves are known to read obituaries and even check times of funerals to identify homes to target for burglaries. If the home is going to be vacant for any time period, you may want to ask the local police department to keep an eye on the property.

You'll want to find all the keys to any property, including storage sheds or lockers, garages, barns, and other outbuildings. It's a good idea to also locate all the other people who may have spare keys. You may want to change the locks so that no unauthorized person has access. Neighbors and even family members have been known to help themselves to personal items. You've probably heard stories of people swarming in even before the funeral to pick out what they think they should be entitled to or to make sure that they get first pick before someone else does. You don't want any items disappearing before an accurate inventory of belongings is made. Plus, you will want to make sure that the sorting and distributing of personal possessions happens in an orderly fashion according to the wishes of the deceased person.

✓　Assemble copies of the deeds and other documentation of ownership to all real estate

You will want to obtain copies of any deeds to real estate your loved one owned. The deed will tell how the property is titled and thus what is now going to happen to the land's ownership and what you need to do. If you do not have a copy of the deed, you can get a copy from the clerk of the land records in the county where the property is located. You will need to refer to these deeds as you go forward with probate. You should also gather documentation related to any condominiums, time-shares, or other property that may change ownership because of the death.

In addition to the deeds to any commercial property that your loved one owned, you should also locate all the other documents that someone is going to need to take over management of the property. At a minimum, you should assemble the business plans and all contracts, lease agreements, account records, bank statements, and tax records for each commercial property.

Likewise, you'll need copies of leases and other documentation of any rental or investment property. As with any income-producing property, you'll want to locate all business plans, leases, easements, assessments, crop insurance policies, tax records, herd records for any livestock, equipment leases or invoices, and inventory of all equipment.

✓ Obtain a copy of the condominium's master deed and association documents

A condominium is a special form of ownership. Typically, a condominium owner individually owns a specific unit as well as jointly owns with all the other unit owners the common areas such as the public hallways, lobby, and recreational areas. You'll need to locate a copy of the master deed or declaration, which describes the space owned, the common areas, and any restrictions on how the property can be used. A copy of the master deed should be on file in the local courthouse.

You should also have a copy of the condominium association documents. The condominium association includes all the unit owners who manage the condominium through an elected board of directors. The condominium association may also have a separate set of bylaws or rules that set out further details, such as how the condominium is to be managed, pet restrictions, color choices, and how monthly unit fees are assessed. It should also inform you about what needs to be done on the death of the owner.

✓ Review how the property is titled

Real estate can be owned, or "titled," in many different ways. For example, you can own a home in your own name or jointly with others. You can keep the right to live in your home for as long as you live, even after giving ownership to someone else. You can own the space where you live, but not the building, or a trust could own your home. How the home or other real estate is titled has a significant effect on you as a spouse or heir and how the property will be distributed. Each of the five different ways a home can be owned has different legal consequences for the survivors.

Individual Ownership A person can own real property **individually** in his or her own name. He or she alone has the right to sell it, rent it, transfer it by will, and use it in any legal way. The deed would read something like, "Owner conveys to Jane Doe, sole individual, all right, title, and interest to the following property."

Individually owned property in just one name will pass according to the direction in that individual's will. If there is no will, state law of **intestacy** will determine who gets it. Intestacy law sets up a priority scheme of inheritance. To a degree, it tries to anticipate whom the typical person would want to inherit the property if he or she had gotten around to writing a will. Every state can have a different priority list, but usually real estate would first go to a spouse, and if no spouse then to children, and if no children then to parents, then to siblings, and so forth out multiple branches of the family tree to the closest next of kin. The person most closely related to the individual according to the state's priority list will inherit. If there are several individuals in that same relationship, let's say three second cousins once removed, each would inherit a third. Most intestacy laws also include rules of what to do when there are bumps in the family tree such as adopted children, deceased children with living children, or children from multiple marriages. Only if no next of kin can be located does the state get the property, a process called **escheat** to the state.

Joint Ownership There are two ways real estate can be owned with someone else. The specific language used in the deed establishes whether the owners are joint owners or common owners. **Joint owners with right of survivorship** have equal ownership and rights to use and enjoy the property. The deed would read something like, "Owner conveys to Jane Doe and John Doe, jointly with right of survivorship, the following property." When one of the joint owners dies, the surviving owner or owners automatically continue to own the property. The last surviving joint owner ends up as the sole owner of the property. This last owner can then leave that property by will, or it will be distributed through intestacy rules. All surviving joint owners must agree to sell or mortgage the property.

Common Ownership Ownership in common (called tenants in common) is the other primary way to own real estate with someone else. The deed would read, "Owner conveys to Jane Doe and John Doe, as tenants in common, the right, title, and interest to the following property." The key difference is what happens to the share of ownership when a common owner dies. Unlike joint ownership with right of survivorship, the surviving owner does not inherit any greater interest or share in the property than he or she already had. The deceased common owner's share passes to the decedent's estate. It will be inherited according to the terms of the will, or intestacy if there is no will.

Community Property For spouses in ten states (Alaska, Arizona, California, Idaho, Louisiana, Nevada, New Mexico, Texas, Washington, and Wisconsin), all property acquired during the marriage automatically becomes **community property**. The laws vary in each of these states, but the basic theory is that each spouse acquires an equal interest in the property. When a husband or wife dies, only one-half of the marital property is inheritable because the surviving spouse owns in his or her own right one-half of the marital property. Each spouse has the right to assign by will the ownership of his or her portion of the community property. In community property states, property that either spouse brought into the marriage or inherits is considered separate property.

Life Estate A life estate is a special type of property ownership that separates the right to occupy the property from the actual ownership of the property. A property owner can sell or give the ownership of property to another but keep the right to continue to live on the property. This right to occupy is called a **life estate**. The owner of the property that is subject to a life estate can sell the property to someone else, but the new owner cannot occupy the property until the person with the life estate dies. The person with the life estate can stay put as long as she lives. Once the person with the life estate dies, the owner of the property has full ownership rights and can live in it, sell it, or do anything else a property owner can do.

✓ Obtain a copy of any trust documents

In many ways, a trust is similar to a will, but it has several very different and important features. A **living trust** is created when a person, called the grantor or settlor, drafts a document that provides directions as to how the property in the trust is to be managed while the grantor is still alive as well as how the property is to be managed and eventually distributed after the grantor's death. The grantor can pick what property belongs to the trust but must convey ownership of the property to the trust. The deed would say something like, "I, Jane Doe, convey to the Jane Doe 2013 Trust all right, title, and interest to the following property" or, depending on the state, "I, Jane Doe, convey to the trustee of the Jane Doe 2013 Trust all right, title, and interest to the following property."

The grantor retains no ownership of the property. The grantor can, however, retain the right to occupy by naming herself the beneficiary of the trust for as long as she lives. She will also name secondary beneficiaries of the trust who have the right to the property after her death.

Property held in trust will be distributed to beneficiaries according to the terms of the trust document, not according to the terms of the will. For example, if Fred's will says, "Everything I own to Betty" but the house is in trust, Betty does not get the house. The trust owns the house, not Fred. Susan, the secondary beneficiary of Fred's trust, gets the house. Because the grantor does not own the property, any property in a trust is not part of the estate, thus avoiding having that property go through the probate process. One reason people put out-of-state property into a trust is to remove the need to have to go through probate in the second state. Refer to Chapter 11 for more information on the probate process.

✓ Obtain a copy of any time-share contracts

A time-share is a way to own the right to use the property rather than direct ownership of the property. With most time-shares, multiple people have the right to use the same property, with each having a specific period of time when they have exclusive use of the property. Depending on the specific time-share, you may purchase a specific week in a specific unit, be able to negotiate a rotating time schedule, or trade your share for use of multiple properties.

Because there are so many variations on the time-share concept, the contract is very important. It will explain what happens to the time-share on the death of the owner. Again, it's very important to know how title to the time-share is held. If it is held jointly with right of survivorship, the survivor will automatically become sole owner of the time-share; this should be a hassle-free process. If the deceased was the sole owner or held the time-share in common with another family member, it will need to go through the probate process in the state where the time-share is located. If it is in a different state than the deceased's official residence, a second probate process will be necessary. If the time-share is held in a trust, probate is avoided. Ownership would pass by the terms of the will, or intestacy if no will. As the executor, you will be responsible for making sure that any mortgage, time-share upkeep fees, and property taxes are timely paid during the probate process.

A caution about selling time-shares: If you inherit a time-share and don't want to keep it or as executor you need to sell it, getting a fair price may be a challenge. The Federal Trade Commission (FTC) cautions would-be time-share sellers to deal only with reputable resell companies, never pay for a promise of a ready purchaser, get everything in writing first, and pay any fees only after your unit is sold. Check out the reputation and complaint history of any reseller with the Better Business Bureau or the FTC.

Depending on the time-share company, you may be successful if you ask in writing if it will accept a quitclaim deed. With a quitclaim deed, you are relinquishing any rights that you have over the property. With a quitclaim deed you would not receive anything in return, other than possibly getting out of the need to continue to pay the time-share fees and other expenses. In any event, you need to talk with the time-share company to make sure that it will accept the quitclaim deed and whether the estate will be liable for any past or future fees or expenses.

✓ Consult with an attorney about the need to change the title to any property if you are a surviving joint owner

If you have inherited property as a joint owner by right of survivorship, you should talk with a lawyer about whether you should prepare a new deed. The new deed would state that the other owner is deceased and that you are now the sole owner. You don't have to have the new deed to own the property as you obtained full legal ownership because of the way you originally owned the property with another. Having your status as sole surviving owner set forth in a new deed simplifies things when you want to sell the property or when you pass away. It is one of those zillion details you can put off for a while.

✓ Check out the rental agreement

If you and your family member were renting an apartment or have a contract with an assisted living facility, you probably have at least one of two questions. Can you stay in the property and keep the lease? Similarly, can you break the lease and move everything out? As with all matters dealing with property, you need to know what the document says. For rental property, the rental agreement or contract has the answer to what's next.

If you want to stay in the property, the answer depends on (1) if you are already on the lease; or (2) if not, whether you can take over the responsibility of paying the rent. Unless there is something in the lease that requires a certain level of income or ability to pay that you cannot meet on your own, the first answer is yes. If, however, you are not on the lease and you want to stay in the property, it depends on what the lease says about transferring or assigning the rights to the property to someone else on the death of the person whose name is on the lease, called the leasee. If you want to break the lease, the answer again depends on what the lease says about the death of the leasee!

Almost every rental agreement will specify the term of the lease. The term could be month to month, one year, or several years. The term guarantees the renter's right to use the premises for the specified length of time. It also requires the renter to continue to pay the rent until the end of the term. Under most circumstances, it's hard to vacate the premises and stop paying the rent in the middle of the contract. In most contracts, however, the death of the renter is a valid reason to break the lease and stop paying rent. You'll need to read the lease to see whom you need to notify of the death and the intent to vacate the premises. You may need to have the place cleaned up and cleared out by the end of the month, or within 30 days of the death, to avoid having to pay another month's rent.

✓ Stay put for now

Although everyone's situation is unique, the common wisdom is that you should stay in your home following the death of a spouse at least for the time being. Right now, the house may seem too big, too empty, or too difficult to manage on your own. Keeping the lawn mowed, doing the maintenance, shoveling the snow, and keeping it clean may be chores that you are unwilling or unable to face right now. A move to a different-sized home, to a place closer to family, or to a different climate may be the right move for you. Don't be hasty to make such a big decision. Take your time to think through a variety of options and evaluate your financial picture before suddenly pulling up roots.

Real Estate Action Checklists

Commercial or Rental Property

❑   There is no commercial or rental property.

❑   I have identified the following commercial or rental property:

Property address: _____

_____

Township: _____ County: _____

Ownership interest is:

❑   Sole

❑   Community property

❑   Joint with right of survivorship

❑   Tenant in common

❑   In trust

With: _____

The tenant is:

Name: _____

Phone: _____ Fax: _____

Address: _____

_____

E-mail: _____

Condominium

❏   There is no condominium property.

❏   I have identified the following condominium property and have notified the condominium association of the death:

Property address: _____

_____

Township: _____ County: _____

Condominium association can be contacted:

Name: _____

Phone: _____ Fax: _____

Address: _____

_____

E-mail: _____

Ownership interest is:

❏   Sole

❏   Community property

❏   Joint with right of survivorship

❏   Tenant in common

❏   In trust

With: _____

Farmland

- ❏ There is no farmland.
- ❏ I have identified the following farmland:

Property address: _____

_____

Township: _____ County: _____

Ownership interest is:

- ❏ Sole
- ❏ Community property
- ❏ Joint with right of survivorship
- ❏ Tenant in common
- ❏ In trust

With: _____

Rental Agreements

❏ There is no rental agreement.

❏ I have identified the following rental agreement and notified the management of the death:

Property address: _____

_____

Unit: _____

Property manager:

Name: _____

Phone: _____ Fax: _____

Address: _____

_____

E-mail: _____

Term of the agreement: _____

Must vacate by: _____

Residence

❑   There is no residential property.

❑   I have identified the following residential property:

Property address: _____

_____

Township: _____ County: _____

Ownership interest is:

❑   Sole

❑   Community property

❑   Joint with right of survivorship

❑   Tenant in common

❑   In trust

With: _____

Time-share

❑   There is no time-share property.

❑   I have identified the following time-share property:

Property address: _____

_____

Type of share: _____

Ownership interest is:

❑   Sole

❑   Community property

❑   Joint with right of survivorship

❑   Tenant in common

❑   In trust

With: _____

Time-share management company contact is:

Name: _____

Phone: _____ Fax: _____

Address: _____

_____

E-mail: _____

Property management fees are: _____

Property management fees are due on: _____

Real Estate: Other

Other miscellaneous information of interest:

_____

_____

_____

_____

_____

_____

_____

_____

_____

_____

_____

_____

_____

_____

_____

_____

_____

_____

_____

_____

_____

_____

_____

_____

_____

_____

_____

_____

_____

_____

CHAPTER 9

PAY DEBTS

When someone dies, one of your concerns will be what to do about any debts your loved one might owe. You'll need to know how to respond to creditors who are seeking payment, what bills you need to pay, and if you can put off paying any of them. You will have to calculate how much debt there is and who is going to be responsible for making the payments. Whose name is also on the debt may make a big difference.

The responsibility—and liability—for paying debts depends on your legal relationships with the debt and with the loved one's estate. If you are the official executor of the estate, your responsibilities are different from those of a spouse whose name is also on the debt and different from those of a family member who is trying to help settle the loved one's affairs. What you can or must do depends on what "hat" you are wearing.

Not all debts are the same. Some bills may have to be paid before others, especially if there is not enough money to pay all debts. As the executor or personal representative of the estate, you have the responsibility to inventory all the debts and pay them as legally required before you can distribute anything to any of the beneficiaries.

Because not all debts have the same priority for being paid off, the first step is to let all creditors know of the death. This step is important because it stops the running up of interest and late fees while you are inventorying all the debts. If your name is also on the debt or you are the executor, you will need to take steps to make sure that the loans do not go into default while you are settling the estate. It's best to make sure that every party holding a debt knows of the death. You'll need to obtain any waivers or forbearance on debt collection or default.

You shouldn't start paying on any of the debts until you've determined how much total debt needs to be paid and which debts have to be paid first. When there's not enough money in the estate to pay off all debts in full, state law will determine the priority of payment. In most states, medical bills for the final illness and funeral expenses have a high priority to be paid before other types of debts.

Of course, some bills—such as utilities, electricity, and water if the family is still in the home or if the house needs to be kept warm to keep pipes from freezing before it is sold—need to be paid. The court will have a process by which household expenses can be authorized to be paid while the estate is being settled. Check with the estate's lawyer for advice on what can be paid and what to do when or if you or anyone in the family is being harassed by debt collectors.

My to-do checklist

Done   **Need to Do**

Done	Need to Do	
❏	❏	Assemble documentation of all bills and credit card accounts
❏	❏	Determine if there are any other types of debts
❏	❏	Notify all credit card companies
❏	❏	Send a copy of the death certificate to each credit reporting company
❏	❏	Determine how much debt is due
❏	❏	Get credit in your own name if you held joint accounts
❏	❏	Take care of the home mortgage or rent
❏	❏	Make arrangements to pay off the reverse mortgage
❏	❏	Pay attention to any vehicle liens
❏	❏	Complete the checklists for Chapter 9

Pay debts action checklists

The Action Checklists in Chapter 9 are set out in the following order:

- *Commercial Property Debts*
- *Condominium*
- *Credit Cards*
- *Credit Reporting Companies*
- *Farmland*
- *Personal Debts*
- *Residence*
- *Time-share*
- *Pay Debts: Other*

Debts can be of many different kinds and have many different consequences to your loved one's estate and to you personally. Before paying any bill or debt, you need to have a good understanding of the different types of debt and their various legal distinctions. Also, whose name is on the debt or who else might also be responsible to pay the debt can make a difference as to who has the responsibility to make payments.

✓ Assemble documentation of all bills and credit card accounts

It may not be too difficult to miss most bills that are due. Notice of payments due on credit cards, utilities, mortgage payments, rent, phone—the sorts of bills that are routinely due—may quickly fill the mailbox. You should also check for statements or notices as well as automatic online payments that come via e-mail. This process can be the trickiest part of your job. Read more about online accounts and payments in Chapter 10.

You'll need to track down all credit card accounts. You loved one's wallet or billfold is an obvious place to start. A check register or bank statement (paper or online) will give you clues about what credit card accounts need to be notified and frozen. A credit report (from one of the three consumer credit reporting bureaus: Equifax, Experian, or TransUnion) will also list credit card accounts. Check there for accounts that may be open but inactive with no balance.

✓ Determine if there are any other types of debts

In addition to credit card debt and other types of routine bills such as telephone, electricity, and water, you need to find out if your loved one had any other type of debts. He or she may have lent money to a relative, friend, or associate. You'll need documentation of the terms of the **personal loan** so that you know what needs to be paid.

If your loved one intended to forgive any debts at death, that fact needs to be in writing. Such intentions might be stated in the loan document or in the will. The borrower relying on oral promises to forgive the debt will have to prove such promises to the executor and the probate court. Other debt may be in the form of business loans, mortgages on other property besides the home, time-share fees, and condominium payments. To be able to calculate the total amount of debt owed, deadlines for payments, and terms of the loans, you will need to gather all documentation of monthly payments and balances due.

✓ Notify all credit card companies

Most credit card accounts are a form of **revolving credit**, which means in general that the borrower is allowed to borrow up to a maximum amount with the expectation that there will be monthly or periodic payments to reduce the amount owed. As long as charges are kept below the maximum amount, new charges can be made. Also, as long as the amount borrowed is paid off in full the next month, no interest is due. Any amount not paid in full is going to be charged interest. If payments are late, penalties may also be due.

To avoid a rapid increase in the amount owed, you need to call each credit card company as soon as possible to notify them of the death. Ask where to send a certified copy of the death certificate. Once the company learns of the death, interest and penalties stop running up.

Also check to see if the card came with any credit card payment protection plan. Some of the major credit card companies offer for an extra fee to waive some of the balance in the event of the death of the cardholder. The cost for this protection can be high, but if your loved one paid for this coverage, make sure that you don't miss out on the benefit.

You will also want to know where all the credit cards are located and make sure that no one else is still using them to make purchases. Keep all cards in your possession for safekeeping.

✓ Send a copy of the death certificate to each credit reporting company

You'll want to notify the three major credit reporting companies—Equifax, Experian, and TransUnion—of the person's death to make sure that your loved one's file is flagged as "deceased." Send a copy of the death certificate to all three, certified mail with a return receipt, so that you can document that you sent the death notice.

Why is this step important? It is so no further credit can be surreptitiously obtained by an identity thief. As sad as it may sound, identity thieves are known to read obituaries to seek potential victims. One fraud prevention firm estimates that the identities of 2.5 million deceased Americans are used to open credit card accounts, apply for loans, and get cell-phone or other services. Knowing that dead people don't check their credit reports, these thieves believe they can open new accounts with abandon and their actions won't be spotted.

After a few months, check your loved one's credit report with one of the credit reporting companies for no cost at www.annualcreditreport.com to see if there has been any suspicious activity. Several months later, check again at the same site to get another free report from a different credit bureau. You can get one free credit report a year from each of the three bureaus.

✓ Determine how much debt is due

When you notify the credit card companies and other creditors of your loved one's death, it's advisable not to promise to make any payments. What needs to be paid depends on several factors: whose name or names are on the debt, where you live, and how much overall debt is due.

- **Name on the debt:** You'll need to find out exactly who applied for the credit and whether any other names are listed. If the debt or credit card account was solely in your deceased family member's name, the estate will be responsible to pay. If the debt is jointly in your name or someone else's name, you or the other person may be responsible for all the payment or you may be jointly liable along with the estate. You'll have to check the fine print on the credit card company's contract or other documentation of the debt. If you or someone else was an authorized user of a credit card and didn't sign the credit application, you are not liable, but the estate is.

- **Location:** If you live in a community property state, a spouse may be responsible for the debt. Ten states employ community property laws: Alaska, Arizona, California, Idaho, Louisiana, Nevada, New Mexico, Texas, Washington, and Wisconsin. Although each state's laws may be different, you'll need to check with your lawyer to see if you have to pay, even if you were not a joint owner with your spouse on the credit card or other debt.

- **Overall debt:** What if the estate lacks the funds to pay all the debts, including the credit card bills? You (or the executor) must first tally all the assets and all the debts. If there are more debts than assets, some types of debts must be paid in full first before other debts are paid. Debts that are **secured**, such as a mortgage on the

---

Dealing with debt collectors: It's well known—but illegal—that some debt collectors try to harass spouses and family members to pay debts left behind when someone dies. If you were not a joint owner of the credit card or any other type of debt, you are not responsible to pay off the debt, even if the collection company says that you must pay.

Before promising to pay collectors or even before sending any payment from your own account, you need to independently determine if you are in any way liable, if the amount they say you owe is even accurate, and if the time limit (statute of limitations) for having to pay anything has passed.

Debt collectors can be very persuasive and intimidating. They may lie about the amount due or your liability for the debt. They may threaten to harm your credit record and even try to sue you in court. These practices are against the law, but they happen.

Debt collectors are keenly aware that survivors are particularly vulnerable psychologically after the death of a loved one. They may use the time of grieving to convince family members to pay debts that they do not owe. They may be fishing for information about the loved one's finances or randomly calling family members (gleaned from the obituary), trying to find someone who can be talked into paying the debt.

If you get a call from debt collectors, take notes of who is calling, the phone number and address, what collection company the caller represents, and all the details of the debt the caller is trying to collect (creditor, date on the account, amount, names on the account, etc.). Have the caller send proof of the debt to the executor.

Do not give out personal information such as Social Security number, address, or bank account. **Do not give out** any information about other family members or about the deceased. The only question that the debt collector can legitimately ask is who has legal authority to pay the deceased person's bills. Do not answer any other questions, even if the caller sounds friendly or helpful.

Do not agree to pay anything until you have checked with the executor or your lawyer. If the calls continue, have your lawyer write a letter demanding that the collection efforts cease.

---

home or loan on a car, must be paid back with any available money before paying off **unsecured** debt, such as credit cards. If no money is left after paying off the secured debt, the unsecured creditors get nothing. The executor will need to notify the credit companies and other unsecured creditors that the estate is insolvent, and the companies will then write off the debt as a bad loan. Spouses and families do not inherit the debt and do not have to pay it off as long as their names are not on the debt. You'll need to work closely with your lawyer to know what needs to be paid and when.

✓ Get credit in your own name if you held joint accounts

If you are a joint owner on the credit card and you want to keep the account, you'll have to negotiate with the company. You will need to agree to pay the balance. It will be up to the company to determine if it believes that your credit is good enough on your own and what the terms of the new account will be. If the interest rate or any other terms are not to your liking, just close the account.

✓ Take care of the home mortgage or rent

The home mortgage is most likely the most important **secured debt** you need to pay attention to. Note that in some states a mortgage is called a deed of trust. The home's equity may be pledged as security to repay first and second mortgages, a line of credit, or a home equity loan. Whatever type of home secured loan it might be, as with all debt, you will need to check the mortgage document to identify whose name or names are on the loan. Commonly, spouses own their residence—and the mortgage—as joint owners with right of survivorship (also called tenants by the entirety in some states), but it's important to check the exact wording used on both the deed and the mortgage. The joint owner will automatically own the home and most likely will now be fully responsible for payment on the mortgage. When title is held as tenants in common or when other people have signed the note, the outcome is going to be different.

You must notify the lender of the owner's death. The lender may want to verify the surviving owner's ability to continue to make payments. Many mortgage companies provide mortgage life insurance when they make a loan, with insurance premiums included as part of the monthly mortgage payment. Check with the mortgage company to see if there is any mortgage life insurance that would pay some or all of the remaining balance on the mortgage.

If your loved one rented a home, you need to notify the landlord. Whose names are on the lease is crucial, as is the fine print in the lease. Check what the lease says about what happens when one of the occupants dies. Typically, the death of a solo renter is grounds for termination of the lease, but you need to find out how quickly you'll need to clean out and vacate the house to stop the monthly rental payment coming due. If other names are on the lease, those individuals most likely will need to make up the balance of the monthly payment, but they can stay in the unit. They may need to go through another credit check by the landlord to make sure that they can afford the rent.

✓ **Notify the company servicing any reverse mortgage as soon as possible to make arrangements to pay off the loan**

A reverse mortgage is a loan against a home that requires no repayment for as long as the borrower or borrowers live there. When the homeowner dies, sells, or moves away, the loan becomes due. These loans are offered by the Federal Housing Administration to homeowners age 62 and older. These federally insured and regulated loans are called home equity conversion mortgages, or HECMs. An HECM is different from other types of loans because the borrower does not make payments during the term of the loan; instead, he or she makes just one big payment when the loan is due.

Your loved one may have taken out a reverse mortgage if he or she needed to use the equity in the home to help meet daily living or medical expenses. Reverse mortgage borrowers have the option to select whether they want to receive the loan proceeds as a line of credit, as monthly disbursements, or as a combination of fixed and open-ended payments. (Note that reverse mortgage borrowers can no longer select a lump-sum payment.) Depending on the borrowers' circumstances and needs, a reverse mortgage may allow them to stay financially secure at home because they don't have to worry about a mortgage payment.

An eligible homeowner can get a reverse mortgage, like a more common "forward" mortgage, from a private lender (such as a bank) that is secured by the equity in the home. Unlike a traditional mortgage that gets smaller as loan payments are made, the reverse mortgage typically gets larger over time because compound interest on the amount borrowed continues to increase the longer the loan is in place.

When the borrower dies, the entire loan must be paid back, which usually means that the home must be sold instead of being passed on to the family. If the borrower sold the home to a third party to repay the loan before the borrower died, the total debt is limited to the home's value, even if the loan balance had become larger than the home's value. If the homeowner sold the home for less than the outstanding balance of the reverse mortgage, FHA insurance makes up the difference to the lender. The heirs or the estate do not become personally liable for the difference.

If the family wishes to keep the home after the reverse mortgage borrower dies, the estate must pay either 95 percent of the current appraised value or the loan balance, whichever is smaller. The estate has up to six months to pay off the loan. You can get up to two 90-day extensions if you can demonstrate that you are actively marketing the property. Interest will continue to grow on the reverse mortgage, so it is important promptly to make a decision about how the loan is to be paid off or if the house needs to be sold. Check with your lawyer for more details about how to pay back a reverse mortgage.

What if there is a surviving spouse living in the home but he or she is not on the reverse mortgage? For example, suppose that the spouse was younger than 62 when the reverse mortgage was acquired. Under old regulations, he or she was in the same position as other heirs and had to repay the smaller of either the mortgage balance or 95 percent of its current appraised value. This regulation was successfully challenged in court to protect the surviving spouse homeowner from being displaced on the death of the spouse who had the reverse mortgage.

✓ Pay attention to any vehicle liens

You will also need to pay attention to the terms of a vehicle loan, which is a **secured** debt. In the case of a car loan, the car is considered to be security that the loan will be repaid. The lender places a lien on the car, so if the debt is not paid, the lender can repossess the car. The car cannot be sold or retitled in someone else's name until the loan is paid and the lien released.

If the loan is only in the decedent's name, the estate will have to pay the loan. If the car and loan are jointly owned, the joint owner will need to continue to make the car payments. The loan will need to be paid in full before the estate can transfer title to someone else. For example, suppose you know that your husband wanted his car to go to your daughter when he died. Unless the lender is willing to let your daughter take over the payments, the estate will need to pay off the loan and have the lender release the lien before the car can be titled in the son's name.

If there is no lien on the car, go to the department of motor vehicles with a copy of the death certificate. It's usually very simple to get a new title in the joint owner's name. Also, tell the insurance company of the car owner's death. You'll want to make sure that the car is insured until you figure out what to do with it.

While you are at the department of motor vehicles, cancel the deceased person's driver's license to prevent duplicates from being issued to fraudsters. Reread the earlier part of this chapter about identity thieves!

Pay Debts Action Checklists

Commercial Property Debts

❑   There is no commercial or business property.

❑   No money is owed on this property.

❑   I have identified the following commercial or business property debts:

Property address: _____

_____

Township: _____ County: _____

Ownership interest is:

❑   Sole

❑   Community property

❑   Joint with right of survivorship

❑   Trust

❑   Partnership

❑   Corporation

With: _____

Purchase price: _____

Amount due: _____

Lender: _____

Phone: _____ Fax: _____

Address: _____

_____

E-mail: _____

Amount due: _____

Lender: _____

Phone: _____ Fax: _____

Address: _____

_____

E-mail: _____

Amount due: _____

Lender: _____

Phone: _____ Fax: _____

Address: _____

_____

E-mail: _____

Amount due: _____

Condominium

- ❏ There is no condominium property.
- ❏ I have identified the following condominium property:

Property address: _____

_____

Township: _____ County: _____

Condominium association contact:

Name: _____

Phone: _____ Fax: _____

Address: _____

_____

E-mail: _____

- ❏ No money is owed on this condominium.
- ❏ I have identified the following money owed on the condominium:

Condominium association dues are: _____

Dues are due: _____

Lender: _____

Phone: _____ Fax: _____

Address: _____

_____

E-mail: _____

Credit Cards

❑   There are no credit card accounts.

❑   I have located the following credit cards and notified the company of the death:

Name of credit card: _____

Contact phone: _____

Address: _____

_____

Account number: _____

Amount due: _____

Name(s) on account: _____

Name of credit card: _____

Contact phone: _____

Address: _____

_____

Account number: _____

Amount due: _____

Name(s) on account: _____

Name of credit card: _____

Contact phone: _____

Address: _____

_____

Account number: _____

Amount due: _____

Name(s) on account: _____

Name of credit card: _____

Contact phone: _____

Address: _____

_____

Account number: _____

Amount due: _____

Name(s) on account: _____

Name of credit card: _____

Contact phone: _____

Address: _____

_____

Account number: _____

Amount due: _____

Name(s) on account: _____

Name of credit card: _____

Contact phone: _____

Address: _____

_____

Account number: _____

Amount due: _____

Name(s) on account: _____

Name of credit card: _____

Contact phone: _____

Address: _____

_____

Account number: _____

Amount due: _____

Name(s) on account: _____

Name of credit card: _____

Contact phone: _____

Address: _____

_____

Account number: _____

Amount due: _____

Name(s) on account: _____

Credit Reporting Companies

❑   I have notified the following credit reporting companies of the death, delivered a copy of the death certificate, and documented my relationship to the deceased:

   ❑   Equifax
      PO Box 740256
      Atlanta, GA 30374

   ❑   Experian
      PO Box 9701
      Allen, TX 75013

   ❑   TransUnion
      PO Box 2000
      Chester, PA 19022

❑   I have ordered a free credit report from www.annualcreditreport.com to get information about credit card accounts and debts.

Date ordered credit report: _____

Credit reporting bureau: _____

❑   I have ordered another free credit report from www.annualcreditreport.com a few months later to check for identity theft.

Date ordered second credit report: _____

Credit reporting bureau: _____

Farmland

- ❑ There is no farmland.
- ❑ I have identified the following farmland:

Property address: _____

_____

Township: _____ County: _____

Ownership interest is:

- ❑ Sole
- ❑ Community property
- ❑ Joint with right of survivorship
- ❑ Tenant in common
- ❑ Trust
- ❑ Partnership
- ❑ Corporation

With: _____

- ❑ No money is due on the farm.
- ❑ I have identified the following farm debts:

Lender: _____

Phone: _____ Fax: _____

Address: _____

_____

E-mail: _____

Amount due: _____

Lender: _____

Phone: _____ Fax: _____

Address: _____

_____

E-mail: _____

Amount due: _____

Lender: _____

Phone: _____ Fax: _____

Address: _____

_____

E-mail: _____

Amount due: _____

Personal Debts

❑ There are no personal debts.

❑ The following persons or companies are due money:

Name of lender: _____

Contact phone: _____

Address: _____

_____

Amount due: _____

Name(s) on debt: _____

Name of lender: _____

Contact phone: _____

Address: _____

_____

Amount due: _____

Name(s) on debt: _____

Name of lender: _____

Contact phone: _____

Address: _____

_____

Amount due: _____

Name(s) on debt: _____

Residence

- ❏ There is no residential property.
- ❏ I have identified the following residential property:

Property address: _____

_____

Township: _____ County: _____

Ownership interest is:

- ❏ Sole
- ❏ Community property
- ❏ Joint with right of survivorship
- ❏ Tenant in common
- ❏ Trust

With: _____

- ❏ No money is due on residential property.
- ❏ I have identified the following residential mortgages (or deed of trust):

First mortgage lender: _____

Phone: _____ Fax: _____

Address: _____

_____

E-mail: _____

Amount due: _____

Second mortgage lender: _____

Phone: _____ Fax: _____

Address: _____

_____

E-mail: _____

Amount due: _____

Home equity loan lender: _____

Phone: _____ Fax: _____

Address: _____

_____

E-mail: _____

Amount due: _____

Reverse mortgage lender: _____

Phone: _____ Fax: _____

Address: _____

_____

E-mail: _____

Amount due: _____

Time-share

- ❏ There is no time-share property.
- ❏ I have identified the following time-share property:

Property address: _____

_____

Type of share: _____ County: _____

Purchase price: _____

Contact person for time-share company: _____

Address: _____

_____

E-mail: _____

Phone: _____ Fax: _____

- ❏ Annual maintenance fee is $ _____
- ❏ It is due on _____

It is payable to:

Name: _____

Phone: _____ Fax: _____

Address: _____

_____

E-mail: _____

- ❏ No money is due on the time-share.
- ❏ I have identified the following money due on the time-share:

Lender: _____

Phone: _____ Fax: _____

Address: _____

_____

E-mail: _____

Pay Debts: Other

Other miscellaneous information of interest:

_____

_____

_____

_____

_____

_____

_____

_____

_____

_____

_____

_____

_____

_____

_____

_____

_____

_____

_____

_____

_____

_____

_____

_____

_____

_____

_____

_____

_____

_____

CHAPTER 10
SORT THROUGH THE STUFF AND PAPERS

Something needs to be done with all your loved one's personal possessions. Sometimes, this task may only require packing up a suitcase of clothes and a box of personal items. Other times, when it means cleaning out the house, basement, and attic where loved ones had been living for 40 years, it's a monumental undertaking.

Before you start throwing things away or giving things to family, you need to take stock of what your loved one had. Other than cleaning out the refrigerator and stopping the newspaper, you need to go slowly before making decisions about the disposal or distribution of any personal items.

First of all, you need to respect the wishes of your loved one as to what he or she wanted done with personal property. Second, you need to respect the laws about taking inventory and determining the value of the estate's assets. This chapter focuses on the personal items—or stuff—that need to go somewhere, but it does not include things like real estate, financial accounts, and other major assets.

You also may encounter lots of paper: old letters, statements, receipts, warranties, magazines, newspaper clippings, and on and on. Someone is going to have to sort through and determine what's important and needs to be saved and what should be discarded.

As more people spend more time online, they collect stuff called digital assets. These digital assets can be social media content on Facebook or Twitter, photos saved in an online album, music stored on iTunes, an online library of books, or accumulated rewards points for airlines or hotels. These accounts need to be managed as part of the stuff that needs to be sorted.

My to-do checklist

Done   **Need to Do**

Done	Need to Do	
❏	❏	Take photographs of rooms, cabinets, and closets
❏	❏	Identify the valuables and their value
❏	❏	Respect the wishes of your loved one
❏	❏	Set up a system to distribute personal items
❏	❏	Shred the paper
❏	❏	Consider estate sales, garage sales, and donations to charities
❏	❏	Recycle with care
❏	❏	Manage digital assets
❏	❏	Complete the checklists for Chapter 10

Sort stuff action checklists

The Action Checklists in Chapter 10 are set out in the following order:

- *Passwords*
- *Rewards Accounts*
- *Sort Stuff: Other*

✓ Take photographs of rooms, cabinets, and closets

Before you do anything with personal items, take photographs or videos. This step is for your protection, especially if you are the executor. Snapshots of items in the dining room cabinet, the clothes closet, and toolsheds will be useful when making an inventory. Take a video panning each room to capture paintings on the walls and special pieces of furniture. Arrange nice jewelry pieces on a soft cloth on a table for a close-up shot. Don't miss getting photos of special items like silver, antiques, or decorative figurines.

Of course, you don't need to get a photo of every junk drawer and shoebox, but think about the items that potentially have either financial or emotional value, even small things like the framed photos of the grandkids. Someone in the family may want them and wonder what happened to them. With a photographic record, you will be better able to defend against claims that something was missing from the inventory. You can also use the photos if you need to prove value or condition for an insurance claim if something gets stolen.

✓ Identify the valuables and their value

A key responsibility of the executor is to assemble a list of all the assets that belonged to the decedent at the time of death and determine their value. This step is called marshaling or inventorying the assets. Once personal items leave the home, this task gets difficult to impossible to accomplish.

The services of an appraiser may be needed to get an expert opinion about which items are sufficiently valuable to be mentioned in the inventory and what value should be placed on each item. Clothes, pots and pans, and garden tools don't need to be mentioned (or can be lumped together as personal items). On the other hand, the fur coat, hand-blown glass bowl, musical instruments, jewelry, and garden tractor may need to be listed and appraised. We've all watched enough of *Antiques Roadshow* to know that it can take an expert to spot what does or doesn't have value.

Look for receipts for special items to help in the appraisal. Items covered under a rider to a homeowners' insurance policy can indicate value. Canceled checks or credit card statements may show the purchase price to aid in evaluation.

✓ Respect the wishes of your loved one

Once you have a good idea of your loved one's personal items, you can start thinking about what you should do with them. You need to pay close attention to any known wishes of your loved one about who is to get what. Look for a letter of instruction that may be attached to a will. A letter of instruction is not a legal document, but it may contain a list of personal things your loved one wants to go to specific people. You'll want to follow these instructions out of respect for the wishes of your loved one, but you are not legally required to do so. The will may also contain specific bequests of major items. The court will require you to follow the directions in the will.

Rather than a letter of instruction, some people write notes on items they want to go to specific people. Look on the backs of paintings, inside vases, or under tables for directions.

✓ Set up a system to distribute personal items

If you don't have clues about who gets what, you need to come up with an equitable system for distributing personal items. It's important that you get family buy-in to your plan. Each family may come up with a different system. For example, in one family, each of the three children started with a sheet of colored stickers. They drew straws to determine who would choose first in the first room, and then that person placed a sticker on the item in that room he or she most wanted. Each child in turn placed their colored sticker on the item he or she wanted. In the second room, a different child had first choice. Anyone could skip a turn if he or she wanted to conserve stickers for items in a different room. With this system, everyone felt good about getting what they wanted. Your family will have to consider what happens if all the heirs can't participate, how many sheets of stickers to use, or other "rules" to prevent hurt feelings.

The main thing you want to avoid is the "grab and go" or unverifiable claims that "she always wanted me to have this piece." The result of no system is invariably family discord. There are frequent stories of family members who didn't speak to each other for decades because of who did or didn't get the tea set.

You may want to check the advice in "Who Gets Grandma's Yellow Pie Plate?" at www1.extension.umn.edu/family/personal-finance/who-gets-grandmas-yellow-pie-plate.

Marlene Stum with the University of Minnesota Extension Service developed this fun and helpful resource to help families avoid conflict while dividing up personal items.

✓ Shred the paper

One task you'll have to address is what to do with all the paper documents. They could be bank statements, receipts, bills, personal letters, newspaper clippings, canceled checks, and so much more. The paper stuff ranges from very important to junk. Some needs to be kept and organized. A lot of it can probably be discarded.

Before you throw everything into the trash, you need to think through what you need to keep and why you need to keep it. Some papers will be very important for documenting what goes into the inventory and appraisal; other records will be useful in tracking down pension funds or insurance benefits for beneficiaries. Records that will be used in filing the final personal income tax return need to be kept. Receipts for major home improvements are valuable for documenting the gift basis of the home. Old tax returns and the supporting documentation of deductions should be kept for seven years just in case the returns are audited by the Internal Revenue Service (IRS). Use the What to Keep and When to Shred checklist in this chapter for ideas about how long you should keep certain records.

The family will need to come to an agreement about what to do about personal letters, photograph albums, and other items that have sentimental value. Family members may cherish and want to keep for future generations the bundle of letters written while parents were courting or separated during military service. Old diaries may bring back cherished memories, or they may be much too personal to keep. Be sensitive to the wishes of your loved one when determining what to do with these personal items. Legend has it that Martha Washington burned all her correspondence with George to keep it away from prying eyes of both family and the public.

Because of the risk of identity thieves going through the trash to glean personal information about your loved one, shred anything you are discarding that has identifying information, such as account numbers or addresses. One option is to invest in a durable paper shredder for the rest of the paper stuff. If you need industrial-strength shredding done, look in the newspaper or online for local shredding events. Libraries and shopping centers frequently host events at which you can safely and securely shred large quantities of paper.

✓ Consider estate sales, garage sales, and donations to charities

Regardless of the system you use to fairly distribute personal items, mementos, and photographs, stuff will remain. What do you do with all the things no family member wants?

One option is an estate sale, typically held by professionals, as a way to get rid of a whole house full of possessions. Items may be auctioned off in the home, be hauled away to an auction site, or be tagged with a price. In an estate sale, price negotiation for the items is usually an option. The company will take a percentage of the proceeds and may even agree to dispose of things that no one purchases. Be sure to get a signed contract that clearly explains what the company will do, how much it will take in commission and fees, the costs of advertising, liability for accidents at the site, and disposal of unsold items.

Another option is to have auctioneers come to the house to bid on specific items they want to take to their auction site. To make sure that you get the best price, you may want a couple of different companies to view the items and make competitive bids.

You might want to hold a garage sale yourself. You get all the proceeds, but you have to do all the work yourself to set up, negotiate prices, and take care of the leftovers.

Check with consignment shops to see what items they might be able to sell. Consignment shops typically give you a small percentage of any items they sell. Vintage clothing can bring a good price in the right location.

Explore other groups that may be interested in special collections or items. A train museum may be interested in a donation of antique model trains. Books may be donated to a library or local fund-raising book sale or may be sold to secondhand bookstores. Some books may be sold—although not for much money—by the pound to a secondhand bookstore. You may be unsuccessful in finding a home for boxes and boxes of books and may have to haul them away. At worst, you can look for a place to recycle books or put them in the paper recycling box.

✓ Recycle with care

Speaking of recycling, check the Internet for ways to recycle almost anything: paint, tires, scrap metal, electronics, you name it. Your county or local government may have special days and locations to drop off hazardous materials that shouldn't go into a landfill. Your local pharmacy may have a way to dispose of unused medications. Don't flush any medications down the toilet!

Cars, boats, and planes can be donated to charities, although you need to follow IRS rules to determine how much can be deducted. If you want to claim a deduction between $250 and $500, you need a written acknowledgment of the donation with a description of the vehicle from the charity. If you claim more than $500, the charity needs to provide you with Form 1098-C, and you then need to file Form 8283, which includes the vehicle identification number, dates the vehicle was donated and sold, and the gross proceeds of the sale. The deduction is limited to the gross amount of the sale of the vehicle to a third party. For more details, search "car donation" at www.irs.gov.

Other donations of appliances, furniture, and household items can be made to AMVETs, Catholic Charities, Goodwill, and ReStore, a resale store run by Habitat for Humanity. These are just a few of the charities that will take donations of usable, used items.

Be sure to keep receipts or acknowledgments for all charitable donations. The decedent's charitable deductions will be made on his or her personal income tax return for the year of the death.

✓ Manage digital assets

Much of your loved one's life may have been spent on the Internet. There are e-mail accounts, iTunes files, e-books, Facebook, LinkedIn, and Twitter accounts, blog posts, electronic banking, online bill paying, digital photo storage, shopping sites, and airline frequent flyer miles, just to name some of the most obvious.

The biggest hurdles are knowing which accounts you need to attend to and then getting access to the account. Then you need to figure out what you want to do—or can do—with the account. Among all the possible accounts out there on the web, some you may want to close out, others may need to be deleted, and yet others you may want to transfer.

What's out there: If you're lucky, your loved one left a listing of online accounts and their related log-ons and passwords, although even if there is a list, chances are that it's not complete or up to date. To figure out what accounts might be out there, start with what you know about the person and how web savvy he or she was.

A simple search of the person's name on the Internet may reveal social media accounts such as Facebook and LinkedIn. Check with family members for Twitter handles. E-mail accounts will disclose electronic banking accounts, frequent flyer account statements, Facebook invitations, and so forth, but you'll need the e-mail password.

What's the password: Without lists of passwords, you're likely to spend time playing detective or thief. Like an identity thief, you may have to try some obvious passwords, those we've all been told to avoid. Search in the obvious places where passwords might be kept, those places we've also been told to avoid. Use your knowledge of the individual to think like he or she might have when coming up with password ideas.

How to gain access: Just about any service on the Internet requires a username, password, or other personal identifier to gain access. Even with a password, though, you're not always free to control the account. The fine print of the online user agreement may not give you or anyone other than the decedent clear authority to access or manage the account. State and federal laws may also restrict the online service's ability to transfer accounts and may prevent you from retrieving stored information. What you'll be able to do with one account may be totally different with another.

Two federal laws that protect online users' privacy may make it hard for you to gain access as an unauthorized user. The Computer Fraud and Abuse Act governs some unauthorized access to computers, and the Stored Communications Act protects the privacy of information stored on an Internet server from third-party access. Although primarily designed to prevent unauthorized users from gaining access to the files and set criteria for government search warrants, in the end these laws can prevent the server from allowing you to gain access. A few states have passed laws to give some authority to executors to manage digital accounts, but much confusion and many complications still exist.

What to do: You'll have to work through each account, one at a time, to figure out what you need to do about it. You may need to keep some accounts temporarily open. For example, you'll want to keep your loved one's e-mail accounts open so that you can retrieve bills and other documents as well as locate information about other accounts that appear in e-mails that arrive after the death. You may be able to learn about additional accounts when online statements or account balances are posted.

Here are some examples of what you can do, but keep in mind that each account is going to be different.

Financial Institutions Contact the branch manager and have a copy of the death certificate handy. Transferring the money to the proper beneficiaries should be relatively straightforward. Ask the manager about direct deposits and automatic bill paying that need to be stopped or redirected to another account before the decedent's account is closed. Chapter 5 on banking explains who are the beneficiaries of different types of accounts: individual, joint, convenience, and pay on death.

E-mail and Social Media

- **Facebook:** Facebook will not reveal the log-in information. A family member can request that the account be closed. It will take a court order in what Facebook openly calls a lengthy process to possibly gain access to Facebook content. The account can be "memorialized" at the request of a "verified immediate family member" at www .facebook.com/help/contact/?id=305593649477238. According to Facebook:
  - No one can log into a memorialized account, and no new friends can be accepted.
  - Depending on the privacy settings of the deceased person's account, friends can share memories on the memorialized timeline.
  - Anyone can send private messages to the deceased person.
  - Content the deceased person shared such as photos and posts remains on Facebook and is visible to the audience it was shared with.

- **Gmail:** Instructions for applying for the content of a Gmail account can be found at https://support.google.com/mail/answer/14300?hl=en. Note that Google says that it is "rare" to release content, and it does so only after a careful review and a lengthy, two-step process with multiple waiting periods.

- **iTunes:** The licensing agreement with iTunes gives the account holder the right to use the content on a specific device, but not to pass the files on to someone else. According to Apple's terms of service, "You may not rent, lease, lend, sell, transfer, redistribute, or sublicense the Licensed Application and, if you sell your Mac Computer or iOS Device to a third party, you must remove the Licensed Application from the Mac Computer or iOS Device before doing so." Any unused balance in an iTunes account is not transferable. These media files are not like a print book or CD that can be physically handed over. If you have access to the computer and to the password, you might be able to access the library. Some media sources suggest that contacting customer service at Apple may be helpful in gaining access to the files.

- **MSN Hotmail:** Compared with some other sites, the process for next of kin to gain access to a loved one's Hotmail account is relatively straightforward. You need to contact the Windows Live Custodian of Records by e-mailing msrecord@microsoft .com to initiate the process. You'll find the documentation you need to process your request at http://answers.microsoft.com/en-us/windowslive/forum/hotmail-profile /my-family-member-died-recently-is-in-coma-what-do/308cedce-5444-4185 -82e8-0623ecc1d3d6.

- **Yahoo:** Right to Yahoo contents ends on death. The e-mail account may be deleted by submitting a copy of the death certificate.

Airlines

- **American Airlines:** AAdvantage miles can be transferred out of a deceased member's account to a beneficiary's AAdvantage account. On request, the airline will send a packet with an affidavit that the beneficiary should fill out. It should be signed by the surviving spouse, the sole heir, or the executor of the estate. A copy of the death certificate must also be submitted.

- **Delta Airlines:** Delta changed its policy in 2013 and no longer allows rewards points to be transferred after death.

- **Southwest:** RapidRewards points cannot be transferred once a member dies. Family members who know their loved one's account number and password may be able to book tickets within two years of the last reward activity.

- **US Airways:** Dividend Miles can be transferred to a survivor's account free of charge as long as the request is made within a year of the member's death and the account was active when that person died. You must submit a will or other legal document establishing survivorship as well as a copy of the death certificate.

What to Keep and When to Shred

These documents should be located and kept until the estate is settled:

- **Appraisals**
- **Adoption papers**
- **Baptismal certificates**
- **Birth certificates**
- **Death certificates**
- **Divorce orders**
- **Employment records**
- **Ethical will**
- **Marriage certificates**
- **Medical records**
- **Military records (DD 214)**
- **Retirement and pension records**
- **Social Security cards**
- **Trusts**
- **Wills and codicils**

These documents should be stored until it is time to be shredded:

- **Bank statements:** Keep for one year after tax returns are filed.
- **Bills/sales receipts:** Keep receipts for high-value items to prove the value for inventory purposes. Keep receipts for any tax- or warranty-related items for one year. All other bills should be shredded as soon as they have been paid.
- **Credit card statements:** Shred unless tax-related. If tax-related, keep for seven years.
- **Home improvement receipts:** Keep until the home is sold; they are important for tax purposes when establishing the cost basis of the home.
- **Homeowners' insurance policy:** Keep until the home is sold.
- **Investment records/IRA statements/brokerage statements:** Keep for seven years after your loved one's death and after the account is closed. Keep quarterly statements until you get an annual statement; then compare the statements and shred the quarterly ones.
- **Leases:** Keep until the property is vacated and you have received the security deposit back from the landlord.
- **Life insurance policy:** Keep until the policy is paid plus three years.

- **Mortgage statements:** Keep until the mortgage is paid off plus seven years.
- **Passport:** Shred.
- **Paychecks/pay stubs:** Keep for one year or until the last W-2 is received.
- **Tax returns and related documents:** Keep for seven years, including all accompanying documents such as W-2s and receipts.
- **Vehicle records:** Keep until the car, boat, or motorcycle is sold.

Sort Stuff Action Checklists

Passwords

❏   I have identified the following passwords:

Place: _____

Website: _____

User ID: _____

Password: _____

Personal identification number (PIN): _____

Place: _____

Website: _____

User ID: _____

Password: _____

Personal identification number (PIN): _____

Place: _____

Website: _____

User ID: _____

Password: _____

Personal identification number (PIN): _____

Place: _____

Website: _____

User ID: _____

Password: _____

Personal identification number (PIN): _____

Place: _____

Website: _____

User ID: _____

Password: _____

Personal identification number (PIN): _____

Place: _____

Website: _____

User ID: _____

Password: _____

Personal identification number (PIN): _____

Place: _____

Website: _____

User ID: _____

Password: _____

Personal identification number (PIN): _____

Place: _____

Website: _____

User ID: _____

Password: _____

Personal identification number (PIN): _____

Place: _____

Website: _____

User ID: _____

Password: _____

Personal identification number (PIN): _____

Place: _____

Website: _____

User ID: _____

Password: _____

Personal identification number (PIN): _____

Place: _____

Website: _____

User ID: _____

Password: _____

Personal identification number (PIN): _____

Rewards Accounts

❑ There are no travel rewards accounts.

❑ I have identified the following rewards accounts:

Airline: _____

Account number: _____

Rewards balance: _____

Website: _____

❑ I have notified the company of the death.

❑ I have inquired about transfer policies.

Airline: _____

Account number: _____

Rewards balance: _____

Website: _____

❑ I have notified the company of the death.

❑ I have inquired about transfer policies.

Airline: _____

Account number: _____

Rewards balance: _____

Website: _____

❑ I have notified the company of the death.

❑ I have inquired about transfer policies.

Airline: _____

Account number: _____

Rewards balance: _____

Website: _____

❑ I have notified the company of the death.

❑ I have inquired about transfer policies.

Train: _____

Account number: _____

Rewards balance: _____

Website: _____

❑ I have notified the company of the death.

❑ I have inquired about transfer policies.

Hotel: _____

Account number: _____

Rewards balance: _____

Website: _____

❑ I have notified the company of the death.

❑ I have inquired about transfer policies.

Hotel: _____

Account number: _____

Rewards balance: _____

Website: _____

❑ I have notified the company of the death.

❑ I have inquired about transfer policies.

Hotel: _____

Account number: _____

Rewards balance: _____

Website: _____

❑ I have notified the company of the death.

❑ I have inquired about transfer policies.

Rental car: _____

Account number: _____

Rewards balance: _____

Website: _____

❑   I have notified the company of the death.

❑   I have inquired about transfer policies.

Rental car: _____

Account number: _____

Rewards balance: _____

Website: _____

❑   I have notified the company of the death.

❑   I have inquired about transfer policies.

Rental car: _____

Account number: _____

Rewards balance: _____

Website: _____

❑   I have notified the company of the death.

❑   I have inquired about transfer policies.

Sort Stuff: Other

Other miscellaneous information of interest:

_____

_____

_____

_____

_____

_____

_____

_____

_____

_____

_____

_____

_____

_____

_____

_____

_____

_____

_____

_____

_____

_____

_____

_____

_____

_____

_____

_____

CHAPTER 11
GET READY FOR PROBATE

Whether you are the spouse, son, daughter, next of kin, personal representative, administrator, executor, or trustee, you should know the basics of what it means to "settle an estate" or "go through probate."

The word *estate* brings to mind mansions, fancy cars, and lots of money, but don't be fooled. Anyone with a home, car, bank account, investments, or even a set of nice china or silver has an estate.

What someone owns at the time of death can be grouped into different categories depending on various factors. In the very broadest category is the "estate," which is everything that a person owns at the time of death. There's the **probate estate**, which includes those things that will be distributed according to the will or, if there is no will, according to the state's law of probate distribution. There could also be the **trust estate**, which would include all property that the decedent placed into a trust through a living trust. Then there is the **taxable estate**, which includes those assets that the federal or state government can tax. As you settle the "estate" or the affairs of your loved one, it is essential that you appreciate and understand the differences. Not everything in the estate is part of the probate estate; anything in the trust estate is not part of the probate estate; and not everything in the estate, the probate estate, or the trust estate is subject to taxes.

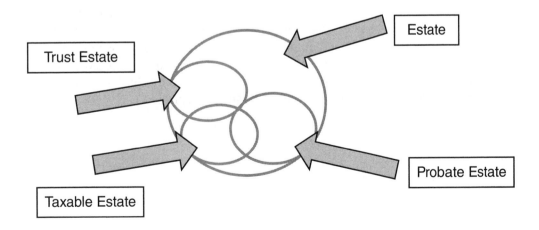

My to-do checklist

Done **Need to Do**

Done	Need to Do	
❑	❑	Inventory all the assets
❑	❑	Determine how assets are owned
❑	❑	Know what to do if there's a living trust
❑	❑	Follow any letter of instruction
❑	❑	Get acquainted with the probate process
❑	❑	Locate the will
❑	❑	Document any major financial gifts
❑	❑	Engage the services of an attorney
❑	❑	Complete the checklists for Chapter 11

Get ready for probate action checklists

The Action Checklists in Chapter 11 are set out in the following order:

- *Codicils*
- *Gifts*
- *Letter of Instruction*
- *Living Trust*
- *Will*
- *Get Ready for Probate: Other*

✓ Inventory all the assets

Before you can plan for the distribution of your loved one's estate, you need to know everything he or she owned, such as bank accounts, investments, personal property, and real estate, as well as everyone he or she owed money to, for mortgages, debts, credit cards, medical bills, funeral expenses, and the like. You also need to know how your loved one owned the assets. Then all the assets have to be categorized as to whether those assets are in the probate estate or are distributed outside of probate. The taxable assets, if any, also have to be categorized so that any applicable tax can be calculated.

Filling out all the checklists in the previous chapters is crucial to completing that inventory. You have to assemble all that important information before you can start making decisions about what to do next in settling your loved one's financial affairs.

✓ Determine how assets are owned

It may sound like an oxymoron, but a probate estate includes everything that the individual previously determined was not part of his or her probate estate. A person does so by owning property jointly with right of survivorship; adding a name to a bank or brokerage account; transferring property into a trust; and indicating a beneficiary of life insurance, annuities, investment accounts, or retirement funds. Many people may not realize that they are doing estate planning—and "avoiding probate"—when they add a name to a deed, own a car with another, or have a joint bank account.

Review the material in Chapter 5 on banking and Chapter 8 on real estate and the information you collected on the checklists about how assets were owned. Property held individually is in the probate estate category, as is property held as tenants in common, but property held jointly is not part of the probate estate. Joint bank or investment accounts and life insurance with a named beneficiary are not part of the probate estate. A second home or any other property held in a trust is not part of the probate estate.

The reason probate is necessary is because there needs to be some legal way to get assets and property out of the ownership of the deceased person and into the hands of the next person entitled to it. The dead person can't do it, so someone needs to be authorized to do so. Co-owners or joint owners already "own" the asset, so they don't need further legal authority to act.

The probate estate will be distributed according to the directions in the will or, if there is no will, according to the distribution laws in your loved one's state. The typical distribution priority would be something like all to the spouse, and if no spouse, then to the children, and if no surviving children, then to surviving parents, then to siblings, then to nieces and nephews, and so on out the branches of the family tree until the nearest surviving heir is found. The listing can be very detailed and convoluted to account for blended families, adopted children, domestic partners, common-law marriages, and all the various combinations of family arrangements. Check with an attorney in your state to find out what happens when there is no will.

Only when no surviving heir can be found does the estate **escheat** to the state. In other words, in those cases, all unclaimed property goes to the state.

Myth busters: It's a myth that if there is no will, the state gets the property. It's also a myth that you don't have to go through probate if there is no will.

If there is a will, the person is said to die **testate**; without a will, they die **intestate**. All assets that are not part of the probate estate will be distributed according to the terms of the documents establishing that asset.

✓ Know what to do if there's a living trust

Property held in a living trust is not part of the probate estate, but it still needs to be managed. A living trust is a legal arrangement in which the **grantor** transfers his or her interest in property so that it can be managed on behalf of the grantor. It is called a living trust because it is created while the grantor is still alive. The trustee whom the grantor selects has the responsibility to manage the trust assets while the grantor is alive as well as after the grantor's death. In addition to creating the trust document, the grantor must also "fund" the trust by preparing deeds, retitling assets, reassigning brokerage accounts, or taking other steps to transfer ownership of the property that the grantor wants in the trust. Because the grantor must transfer legal ownership to the trust, the property in the trust no longer legally belongs to the grantor and therefore is not part of the probate assets.

Every trust has three parties: the grantor, the trustee, and the beneficiary or beneficiaries. The same individual can be all three at the same time. Many people who create a living trust (also called a settlor or donor) name themselves as the trustee because they want to manage the trust as long as they can. They also name a successor trustee who takes over the trust management when the grantor is no longer willing or able to be the trustee and then after the grantor's death. The grantor can also name himself or herself as the principal trust beneficiary; that way, the grantor can receive the trust proceeds to support himself or herself while still alive. The grantor would also name secondary beneficiaries with instructions on when and how the trust assets are to be held and distributed after death. In this way, a trust serves a very similar purpose to a will in identifying how any trust assets are distributed to the named beneficiaries. Because any assets transferred to the trust are not part of a probate estate, the trust, rather than the will, controls how those assets are distributed.

On the death of the grantor, the successor trustee has the responsibility to follow the instructions in the trust on how to manage and distribute the trust property to the secondary beneficiaries. In many ways, the responsibility of the trustee is very much like that of the executor. Each has distinct instructions about what to do with specific property. The

---

When is a trust not a trust? To be an effective document, the creator (or grantor) of the trust must transfer title to the trust of any asset he or she wants to be placed into the trust. AARP is aware of "living trust scams" in which individuals have paid for the boilerplate trust document but not been advised of the need to "fund" the trust. They may have thought that they were doing the right thing to create the trust, but actually they have a worthless—but expensive—legal document. Some of the scammers may have even promoted the trust preparation as in some way authorized by AARP, which is untrue. You'll need to talk with a lawyer if you have any questions about the validity of a trust document.

trustee, however, is responsible only for managing and then distributing the trust property. How much is trust property depends on what assets the grantor decided to put into the trust. Usually, the executor is responsible for everything that isn't trust property or assets that have a designated beneficiary.

Depending on the terms of the will and of the trust, the trustee and executor will need to appraise property, sell or invest assets, file taxes, prioritize debts, hire professionals, and keep beneficiaries informed. The trustee's administrative expenses will be similar to the executor's expenses, and the trustee is entitled to fees for his or her services.

✓ Follow any letter of instruction

A **letter of instruction** serves as guidance to you as a family member or personal representative about matters you must attend to after your loved one's death.

This informal document can be attached to the will, but it is not an official part of it. Although it doesn't carry the legal weight of a will and is in no way a substitute for one, a letter of instruction clarifies any special requests your loved one wants you as a family to carry out. Think of it as a flexible, informal supplement to the will that covers more personal information than what is typically included in a will. Just as with all other estate-planning documents, you should take special care to locate it and follow the wishes expressed in the letter of instruction.

A letter of instruction can have two parts that do two different things. The first part helps you as family know how to find the information necessary to plan the funeral. The letter might include instructions about the type of funeral or memorial service desired, who should officiate, who should be asked to be pallbearers, or what songs should—or should not—be sung. The letter should tell you about plans that have already been made with the funeral home of choice and whether any of the funeral arrangements have already been paid for. You could find a description of the location of any prepurchased burial plot or crypt and where the plot deed is located. It may state if your loved one wanted to be cremated and where to place the ashes.

The other part of a letter of instruction may help eliminate family feuds over who should receive specific personal items. We all have heard stories of family fights erupting over how to divide family pictures, necklaces, the stamp collection, fishing tackle, a figurine set, or the wedding gift from Aunt Sue. The items may not have monetary value, but getting them to the right person can make a big difference to the whole family. If the letter of instruction includes directions on how personal items are to be distributed, be sure to faithfully carry out those wishes.

✓ Get acquainted with the probate process

Probate is the court procedure that determines the validity of a will (if any), determines who will be in charge of settling the affairs, identifies the heirs, inventories the probate assets, determines claims against the estate, and distributes the remaining proceeds to the proper persons. In effect, the probate court makes sure that the individual's wishes as expressed in the will are carried out, supervises how the probate estate is distributed, settles any disputes over the terms of the will or claims against the estate, and sorts out family disagreements. The court will also hear arguments, if any, about the validity of the will, such as claims that there was undue influence over the individual when he or she wrote the will.

Because each state's probate process is different, this discussion is a general introduction to what you might expect as you proceed to settle an estate. Your experience with probate will depend on a variety of factors, such as how well your loved one planned his or her affairs, how much documentation is readily available, how complicated the financial affairs are, how many different types of assets need to be managed, whether there is a trust, how much money is involved, how many creditors have claims against the estate, and how well the survivors get along.

Personal Representatives, Executors, and Administrators If you have been named in the will as the person your loved one wanted to be in charge of managing the estate, the court will most likely appoint you as the **executor**. The exception might be if you are unable to carry out the responsibilities or if you are shown to be unfit for the task. If there is no will in which an executor is nominated, the court will appoint an **administrator**. The duties of the **personal representative**, whether called an executor or administrator, are the same.

Being a personal representative can be a big task that requires good financial skills, attention to detail, patience, and probably a dose of diplomacy. As a personal representative, you must inventory all assets, have them appraised, pay bills, publish legal notices, prepare (or have prepared) the final income tax return, work with financial institutions to close out accounts, record documents to sell or transfer real estate, find and notify beneficiaries, file any estate tax returns, and file inventories and accountings with the court. All the while, you must keep the anxious and impatient debtors and beneficiaries of the estate happy.

Costs and Fees Much has been written about the cost of probate, with people suggesting that probate is a detrimental process that should be avoided at all costs. In reality, settling the estate, with or without probate, is just about the same amount of work, hassle, and expense. Settling the estate does incur fees and costs that cannot be avoided. Some minor costs of the probate process include filing fees to open the probate case and file the will with the court and publishing legal notices in newspapers. Some states may also charge filing fees for the inventory or accountings.

The court may require you as the personal representative to post a surety or faithful performance bond. The purpose of the bond is to safeguard the estate against misuse or abuse. You would pay a small percentage of the value of the probate estate, or whatever amount the judge requires, to a bonding company. In the event that the court finds that you have abused your responsibilities, the court would order the bonding company to reimburse the estate. Many times, people write into their will that they waive the requirement for their executor to post a bond.

The major expenses in settling an estate—with or without probate court involvement—are professional fees for an attorney, real estate agent, appraiser, accountant, or tax preparer. The attorney for the estate advises the personal representative, assists in filing court documents, and represents the estate in any disputes. These professional fees will be paid as an expense of the estate. The more complex the financial affairs are, the higher the professional fees will be.

Depending on the laws of your state, as personal representative you can be paid a percentage of the inventory value of the estate or a set fee determined by the judge. States that use a percentage to calculate the fee typically use a sliding scale. As the size of the estate increases, a smaller percentage is taken from the greater portions of the estate. For example, a personal representative might be entitled to a fee of 5 percent on the first $10,000 of a probate estate, 4 percent of the next $25,000, 3 percent of the next $50,000, and 2 percent of anything over $85,000.

In other states, the personal representative's fee is based on what would be "just and reasonable" compensation for the amount of work the representative has to do. The amount of work involved for a personal representative can differ considerably, even for estates of the same value. It is much simpler to administer an estate if assets can be readily found, no claims against the estate need to be resolved, and no family squabbles need to be negotiated.

Time to Complete Probate A very common question is how long this process will take. The answer depends on many factors. A small probate estate with a jointly owned house, a joint bank account, and a car that needs a new title could be settled in a week with nothing needing to be filed with the court. A multimillion-dollar estate with lots of different kinds of assets; property in several states that needs to be sold to satisfy mortgages, debts, or taxes; challenges to the capacity of the testator at the time that the will was created; and siblings who think that they are entitled to more are all possible situations that separately or in combination have the potential of adding years to the process.

✓ Locate the will

A will, or last will and testament, is the legal document by which someone determines who they want to receive their probate property. In a will, you can leave assets to friends or significant others who are not related to you. By having a will, you can also make sure that someone (other than your spouse) who would inherit if you don't have a will does not do so. You can also make bequests to charities that would not happen if you don't have a will.

A will also names the person whom the **testator** wanted to be the **executor** of the estate. It can name the guardian of any minor children until they reach the age of majority. If the will leaves assets to any minors, such as grandchildren, it may provide for the creation of a testamentary trust so that their inheritance can be managed until they reach the age of majority. A **testamentary trust**, unlike a living trust, is set up as part of a will and comes into effect after the death of the testator. The testator may also make donations or **bequests** to favorite charities, schools, or religious groups and take advantage of tax laws that encourage private philanthropy.

Where are you going to find the will? Ideally, your loved one has let someone in the family know that there is a will and where it is located. Otherwise, first check obvious places, such as a desk drawer or filing cabinet that houses other important papers. It may be kept in a safe-deposit box, but read Chapter 5 about the steps that you may have to take to gain access to the box. The lawyer who drafted the will may be safekeeping it.

A word of caution: In most states, only the signed original will can be probated; copies will not be accepted. Similarly, strikeouts, erasures, and any other markings on the will can have the devious effect of invalidating the entire will. A **codicil** is an amendment to the will that changes specific sections of the will. To be valid, a codicil must be executed with the same formality, number of witnesses, and notary requirements as the original will.

✓ Document any major financial gifts

As personal representative, you will need documentation of any gifts your loved one made during his or her lifetime to be able to determine if any estate tax is due. The Internal Revenue Service (IRS) considers any gift to be taxable unless it falls within four specific exceptions:

- Gifts to a spouse without gift tax consequences
- Gifts of tuition or medical expenses for another if the money is paid directly to the institution or provider
- Annual gifts of less than $14,000 (in 2013) per individual*
- Gifts to political organizations and qualifying charities

All other gifts for less than the item's fair market value should have been reported to the IRS in the year that the gift was made. The IRS considers the laws on gift taxes to be among the most complex in the tax code, so seek professional advice about how to treat any gifts.

Most people will not have to worry about federal estate taxes. As of December 2013, the amount that an individual can exclude from estate taxes, including gifts given during one's lifetime, is $5.25 million. A married couple's exclusion is $10.5 million. These amounts may slightly increase in 2014 and later years.*

States may also have their own estate or inheritance taxes. Generally, they take a smaller percentage than the IRS. Laws vary, however, so check with a local tax expert.

Note: Congress frequently revisits gift and estate tax laws. Check with an estate planning or elder law attorney for current tax provisions.

✓ Engage the services of an attorney

Some states make it fairly easy to settle small estates (defined as less than $75,000 of probate property in Florida and less than $25,000 in Tennessee, for example) with less time and hassle than the process of settling large estates. If most of the property was held jointly, it may be not very difficult to do the inventory, file the reports, and get approval to distribute some assets. Even with small estates, though, it may be wise to consult with an experienced attorney. Paying for a couple of hours of guidance through the process may save you much frustration than if you try to settle all the details on your own.

Get Ready for Probate Action Checklists

Codicils

❑ There are no codicils.

❑ I have identified the following codicils:

Codicil date: _____

Executor (if changed): _____

Phone: _____ E-mail: _____

Address: _____

_____

Witness name: _____

Phone: _____ E-mail: _____

Address: _____

_____

Witness name: _____

Phone: _____ E-mail: _____

Address: _____

_____

Gifts

❑   There are no known gifts in excess of $14,000 per individual per year.†

❑   I have identified the following gifts in excess of $14,000:

Gift to Whom	Date	Gift	Value

---

† *The annual gift exclusion changes from year to year. The exempt amount prior to 2002 was $10,000; for 2002–2005, it was $11,000; for 2006–2008, it was $12,000, and for 2009–2012, it was $13,000. In 2013, it increased to $14,000.*

Letter of Instruction

❏ There is no letter of instruction.

❏ I have identified a letter of instruction.

❏ I have followed the directions in the letter of instruction.

Living Trust

❑   There is no living trust.

❑   I have located a living trust.

Trustee's name: _____

Phone: _____ E-mail: _____

Address: _____

_____

Successor trustee's name: _____

Phone: _____ E-mail: _____

Address: _____

_____

Secondary beneficiary's name: _____

Phone: _____ E-mail: _____

Address: _____

_____

Secondary beneficiary's name: _____

Phone: _____ E-mail: _____

Address: _____

_____

Secondary beneficiary's name: _____

Phone: _____ E-mail: _____

Address: _____

_____

Will

- ❑ There is no will.
- ❑ I have identified a will.

Attorney's name: _____

Phone: _____ E-mail: _____

Address: _____

_____

Executor's name: _____

Phone: _____ E-mail: _____

Address: _____

_____

Witness name: _____

Phone: _____ E-mail: _____

Address: _____

_____

Witness name: _____

Phone: _____ E-mail: _____

Address: _____

_____

The original of the will is located: _____

Get Ready for Probate: Other

Other miscellaneous information of interest:

_____

_____

_____

_____

_____

_____

_____

_____

_____

_____

_____

_____

_____

_____

_____

_____

_____

_____

_____

_____

_____

_____

_____

_____

_____

_____

_____

CHAPTER 12
TAKE CARE OF YOURSELF

The death of a loved one can take a toll on the health of the family survivors. Each of you has been grieving in your own way, perhaps not sleeping or eating well, and worrying about taking care of all the details mentioned in the previous chapters. The stress on the body caused by such a loss can even make you physically sick. It can affect your ability to concentrate or pay attention. A death in the family is rightfully called a major life event that can result in lasting disruptions to psychological well-being as well as to personal and financial circumstances. Grief follows no timetable; you could be getting along fine and then be hit with another bout weeks or months later. Be alert to the toll that grief can take on your body and spirit and then take steps to recovery.

During the weeks and months to come, it's important to take care of yourself. Just taking a walk or a drive in the country can offer a break. Make some time for solitary reflection. It might be calming to visit the cemetery or a house of worship. Now might not be the right time, but start thinking about what you'd enjoy doing the most to pamper yourself.

My to-do checklist

Done   **Need to Do**

Done	Need to Do	
❑	❑	Manage your stress
❑	❑	Get support
❑	❑	Plan a break
❑	❑	Take care of your health
❑	❑	Organize your own life

Take care of yourself action checklists

This chapter has no checklists.

Taking care of yourself includes putting aside all the to-do lists. Make time to do what you want to do, not what you have to do.

✓ Manage your stress

Dr. Elizabeth Harper Neeld, author of *Seven Choices*, recommends the following ways to relieve the stress caused by grief:

- Take sufficient time off from work
- Eat as well as you can
- Drink water
- Loaf and rest
- Move your body: a walk, bike ride, swimming
- Get massages
- Listen to music
- Simplify your schedules
- Cut out activities that take up time and energy you don't have now
- Pray and meditate
- Talk to a professional

Dr. Chris Rothman of the Center for Grief Recovery suggests that you try some of these stress relievers:

- Lie in the sun streaming in through your windows. Bathe and breathe in the sun.
- Designate an afternoon or evening and turn the phone off.
- Set up a specific time of the day to "worry" for 20 minutes. Set a timer. When the time is up, do something to reward yourself.
- Do something you're good at. It is important to ground yourself in your skills and abilities, even if the outcome isn't up to par.
- Comfort yourself by taking a warm bath using your favorite scents and burn aroma-therapy candles. It's invigorating and relaxing at the same time.
- Buy yourself or your loved one a gift and have the clerk gift wrap it to celebrate fond memories.
- Wrap up in a warm blanket. Put on relaxation tapes and sip your favorite tea or hot chocolate.
- Dressed in comfortable clothing, find a rocking chair and rock your troubles away.
- Play music that matches your mood. Feel understood by the songs and singers who share your experiences.
- Especially when you are feeling stressed and overwhelmed, forget about making to-do lists. Instead, at the close of each day, make a list of what's been done.
- Find something alive to care for, such as a plant or a pet.
- Eat at least one nourishing meal each day, even if the food doesn't hit your taste buds like you're used to.

- Make a fire in the fireplace and do some stretching and focus on yourself. You can add your favorite soft music if you wish.

- Breathe, really breathe! Take deep breaths in through the nose and exhale slowly out through the mouth.

- Say "no" to something and "yes" to yourself.

- Try gentle exercise like yoga, tai chi, or walking.

- Spend some time in nature.

- Make a memory box, collage, or journal to store your thoughts and memories.

Be creative when thinking about the best way for you to take a break and take care of yourself.

For more information, see AARP's *Juggling Work and Caregiving*, by Amy Goyer, available free at www.aarp.org/CaregivingBook, which devotes a chapter to caring for yourself.

✓ Get support

You may want to get some professional counseling. Grief counselors or bereavement groups can help you deal with your emotions and get your life back on track. It may be in a different direction from where you were heading before the loss, but counseling can help you go from disorientation to rebalancing your life.

Your faith leader or doctor may be able to help you find individual or group sessions in your area. If your spouse died, ask friends for recommendations of support groups for widows or widowers. If you are now caring for young children without the help of your spouse, you could check out other groups such as Parents Without Partners. Your local area agency on aging is a good place to inquire about appropriate groups or activities that would help you make new friends or just get out of the house.

✓ Plan a break

You may not be able now to get away from all your responsibilities, but start to plan a break. You could plan a long weekend, schedule a session at a spa, or just make an appointment to get your hair cut. If you enjoy fishing, get out your rod and tackle and head for the lake. Figure out a way to get a change of scenery to refresh yourself.

✓ Take care of your health

Part of taking care of yourself is making sure that you stay healthy. Eating right and getting exercise are important for everyone, but they become essential when you are stressed. Because of the physical toll that mourning can have on your body, it's a good idea to make an appointment for a physical exam. It could even be scheduled for a couple of months from now if you don't have any chronic conditions that you're already treating. Don't forget to schedule any other doctor's and dentist's appointments you may have put off.

✓ Organize your own life

Closing out the matters involved in a loved one's life is not simple. Life and lives can be so complicated. You've now experienced how overwhelming it can be to try to locate, organize, sort, discard, share, or distribute all the details about someone else's life. You may be saying to yourself that you don't ever want to put your family through these hassles when you die. You can start to get your own details in order by using *The ABA Checklist for Family Heirs*. Use the checklists in the book or on the CD-ROM to save in one place information about yourself, your personal history, account numbers, passwords, and advance care plans. Help other family members get organized, too. It's a great gift to all your loved ones.